*To Jell*

# FEET

## A chronicle of places my feet have taken me in eighty seven years

*James E. Martin*

By James E. Martin

authorHOUSE®

*AuthorHouse*™
*1663 Liberty Drive*
*Bloomington, IN 47403*
*www.authorhouse.com*
*Phone: 1-800-839-8640*

*First published by AuthorHouse    12/7/2009*

*ISBN: 978-1-4490-0153-7 (sc)*

*Printed in the United States of America*
*Bloomington, Indiana*

*This book is printed on acid-free paper.*

# TABLE OF CONTENTS

# ACKNOWLEDGEMENTS

This book is dedicated to those who have found and never lost the excitement of youth and regardless of age perceive the awesome beauty of the earth as though it is heaven. Each as I have made incalculable numbers of footprints across incalculable miles upon the surface of the earth without giving that activity much thought. Just as each of us has a personal story each has also made an interesting journey. I am so especially grateful that my health and circumstance has enabled me to follow the paths upon which my feet have trod.

JAMES E. MARTIN

# Chapter 1

# FIRST TOYS

One November day late into my eighty-fifth year, I reminded myself that November 29th was the day I had reserved for each of the past twelve years to climb to the top of steep White Rock Mountain near my home at Caldwell, West Virginia. According to my birth certificate, November 29, 1921 was also the date when this little bundle of joy was delivered via stork to Georgia (Nee) Williams Martin, an immigrant from Wales, and Alfred Martin, an immigrant from Scotland.

As always, I made plans for the climb including some heavy socks, comfortable boots, first-aid supplies, bottles of water, some food, and my favorite walking stick. Only once upon a day of glare ice have I unwillingly postponed that climb for twenty four hours. Contemplating that climb caused me to think of many other interesting places which I have visited during what has been a long healthy active life. It also occurred to me that as a matter of convenience, I have always taken my feet with me to every one of them. They have striven to keep pace with me, or have I been busy keeping pace with them?

I do not know if anyone other than a podiatrist has written a book about feet. If so, perhaps not in the manner in which I plan to write this one; a chronicle of most of the places to which my feet have borne me during eighty seven years. I wonder, therefore, if you may be interested in tracking me through these pages to learn what my feet and I have been doing for such a long time. With some exceptions, most of the time has been fun for me.

Since the following narrative is mostly about me, I feel behooved to warn you before you have invested the time needed to read this book, it is an I, I, I, me, me, me book. I can not imagine any other way to tell you the story. I warn you to anticipate an exorbitant reference to I and me throughout.

To get started, both you and I must have a jumping off point, so consider for a moment the first day of each of our lives. Have you ever imagined what your life was like the day of your birth? It actually was one of your most dangerous days, because there was no assurance you were going to survive. Having survived, however, you were destined to live some length of time. The fact that you have just read the opening paragraph of this book affirms that you have survived thus far. Perhaps it is well that you cannot remember that day, for chances are that you were not a 'happy camper.' You had been burped out of a nice warm pouch where all you had to do was absorb nourishment, sleep as long as you wished, had no colic, didn't need a bath, nor did you need dippers changed. Shucks! You didn't even have to breathe. Life was good, but you must have learned quickly that even the good life sometimes encounters bumps in the road. So there you were dumped into a world of bright lights and many noises, having your life line severed, being roughly grasped by your ankles, turned upside down, and punished by being slapped on your behind for no fault of your own. A few seconds ago you hatched and already you are being shown that some events in your new world can make you cry.

Without awareness, however, you immediately had the urge to survive. Your breath began and started making demands upon your parents to satisfy your hunger, provide your need for comfort, safety, acceptance, bonding, clothing, shelter, and cleanliness. Many times, your impatience for those essentials was emphasized by crying tantrums and by frenzied threshing of your arms and legs. Within weeks, you became accustomed to your new environment and began evolving into an appealing little darling who charmed everyone else through your antics, which included cooing and playing with your feet. Have you noticed that infants have the cutest little feet? They are smooth, warm, cuddly, and they tickle when they are touched. The sight of you with one of your big toes tucked coyly inside your mouth was certain to elicit oodles of ooos and aaahs from doting adults and that scene was certain to become a keep-sake inside your family's picture album. I must agree, I'm an avid oooer and aaaher when I am privileged to observe one of those heart warming occasions.

I have written a few other books, so at my book signings, I have observed thousands of infants passing before me riding inside their carriages as they repose upon their backs with their tiny legs extended above themselves and playing with their feet. Although I cannot remember that happening to me, it has occurred to me that eighty seven years ago my feet must have also been my first toys. So I decided to write this book about feet.

Aside from my chassis being too rigid to insert one of my toes into my mouth these days, it is impossible for me to remember having ever been the center of attraction during one of those toe-in-the mouth scenes. Much too frequently, however, I have suffered the humiliation of FITMD which translates into foot-in-the-mouth-disease. I discovered that those occasions were neither heart-warming nor rewarding. When that has happened, I have truly wished that neither of my feet had ever made that journey.

How good is your memory? When she was approximately three years old our first granddaughter who loved visiting her Grandma and me asked, "Papaw, do you 'member' the night I was born?" With hardly a pause, she continued, "Well, I wanted to come home with you guys." Now that is maximum recollection. My memory has not been seriously diminished as the result of my approaching inclusion upon the 'endangered species list', but my recall is not as vivid as hers. Actually, my earliest memories are of days playing in the soft damp earth beneath the family front porch at the age of perhaps eighteen months. Those early days were exciting for me and the journey upon which I hope to take you through the reading of this book continues to be exciting for me to this day.

I do not know if I wore little 'booties' nor can I remember my first lace-up shoes. When our two little granddaughters outgrew their first lace-up leather shoes, I preserved them as keepsakes, each six inches long and a wee bit soiled and scuffed just as they were the last time they removed them from their feet. I was so enamored by them that I felt compelled to write the following to also preserve the magic of that time in our lives:

## FOUR LITTLE SHOES

On a nightstand beside my bed
Next to the pillow where I lay my head
The last things I see when I turn out the light
The first with the dawn of the morning bright
Two pairs of little shoes scuffed and worn
Their first lace-up models after they were born
Our two little granddaughters so lovely and
      sweet

Romped their earliest miles with them
      on their feet
Time capsules of those magic days
A part of our lives which has passed away
But will forever within our memories burn
Time does not stand still, cannot return
Their busy rush across the floor
From room to room and door to door
Silent keepsakes to be worn no more
Ah, those precious days of nevermore

Lovely young ladies now in their prime
Dimly remember that early time
When those little shoes adorned their feet
And they lisped their words as they learned
      to speak
Were intrigued by stories of Brer Rabbit
      and Bear
And wore tiny ribbons in their hair
Rode little trikes with training wheels
Used highchairs and booster seats when
      eating meals

But Time revolves day by day
And other little children may come to stay
At Grandparents' house; we may be called
      Great
Or just plain Gramps as time grows late
In the same old rooms with the same
      old floors
The same old nightstand and the same
      old doors

The two pairs of little shoes that were
    there before
May someday share the space with a few
    pairs more

It was not the wisdom of the Master plan
That the joys of Youth should forsake the
    Land
Thus the rebuilding of nests, the rebirth
    of the rose
The changing of the Seasons as on Time goes
After the harshness of winter comes the
    fresh-ness of spring
Flowers bloom and song birds sing
A Mother smiles as her baby coos
Soon first booties are exchanged for
    lace-up Shoes

Do you too sometimes strive to remember your earliest days? Many to whom I have spoken cannot remember their first school days, others have clear memories when they were two or three years old. Most of their memories are of booster chairs, potty training, cutting baby teeth, learning to talk, how to tie their shoes, and playing 'horsy' upon Daddy's back as he moved across the floor on his hands and knees.

As I have written in my autobiography titled EBBIE and published a few year ago, I did not have the privilege of knowing my parents. Before I reached a cognitive age, my mother died of influenza. For reasons I have never known, my father abandoned me without my ever knowing him. My mother's sister, Blanche, and her husband John Shinosky took me to rear. During my earliest recollections, I believed that they were my parents. They had two young daughters and were also sharing their home with a girl named Annie of perhaps twelve years of age whose parents had also died.

As mentioned in an earlier paragraph, it was the happy memories of playing beneath their front porch at Morgantown, West Virginia where I first became aware of being alive. Many years later, I learned that the house was located upon a one-way hillside street overlooking the first football stadium of West Virginia University at Morgantown, West Virginia.

The cruel realities of hardship and fate did not soon by-pass the family of my benefactors, for near my age of perhaps less than three years, Aunt Blanche also died of the flu. I was too young to comprehend why she was sleeping inside what appeared to me to be strange bed surrounded by flowers, but after a day, she, the bed, and the flowers were gone.

Uncle John was in torment. He had to work, but he could not leave two young daughters, an infant, and a teen aged girl unattended at home. Within days, he entered a marriage to a woman whose first name was Avis. Her husband had recently died in a coal mine accident. She, too, had a daughter near the age of John's daughters. They moved into John's home as a marriage of mutual accommodation. The weeks that followed were times of immense sadness, emptiness, and unpleasant adjustments. The harmony which abounded inside that home changed into the mirthless chill of a morgue. Adjustment came tediously slow as individuals spent long periods silently staring into space. Uncle John's jovial return from work at supper-time each day was replaced by stony silence at the table. Some time each day and after bedtime, I could hear softly audible sobs including my own emanating from dark corners of rooms and beneath the bed covers.

The new house matron's gratitude for her rescue from disaster soon evaporated as she established new rules of conduct in the home. The first was her demand that Annie, the teen-aged girl, would be sent away. Uncle John's sister, Aunt Nell, gladly accepted her as a part of her family. With the attitude that she would only provide a home for John's daughters and hers, his new mate informed him that I, too, must leave. To hasten my departure, she made my life a living hell each day while John was at work and the daughters were at school. I became what can best be described as a nervous wreck. I was no longer permitted to play beneath the front porch, but rather spent the days of the work week confined inside a small dark broom closet beneath the stairway leading from the second floor living quarters and adjacent to the basement kitchen and the outside exit. Being served irregular meals, frequently deprived of toilet usage, and being terrorized by loud banging upon the door of my prison accompanied by threats that demons would devour me, I began having 'nightmares' in my sleep which endured long after my wife and I were married during 1946 following my participation in the U.S. Army of world War II. In addition to that, I began wetting my bed nightly, which caused hostility towards me by my female bedmates.

The end result was that my father reappeared and summoned West Virginia State social workers, aided by deputies, to forcefully remove me from Uncle John's custody. Still shoeless, my feet made tracks inside filthy second floor rooms of a house whose location I have never known. I was totally imprisoned for weeks or possibly months with four other little boys who were also separated from their families and held incommunicado. As to roughly calculate the time we remained there, our hair had grown until we resembled girls. We survived by being rationed a slice of bread and a soup bowl of hot chocolate three times a day in our room during our entire confinement there. Fearing that we were going to die, I instigated a riot and escape by plugging the bathroom sink and tub, turning on the water, and flooding the inside of the house. We escaped when the house mother entered to close the valves. Our bare feet trod upon strange streets for only a short time before we were captured by policemen who must have reported our cruel treatment to their superiors.

It was obvious the following morning that something exciting was forthcoming, because the house mother made an early entrance to our prison, bathed us, and began tidying the rooms. She also raised all windows in an attempt to dispel the heavy stench of lead paint and of urine soaked beds and clothing. She also beseeched us not to reveal any unfavorable comments about our treatment while staying there. In short, she had turned into a defeated whimpering 'pussy cat.'

True to my expectation, the same husband and wife social-worker team who had taken me from Uncle John's home arrived. The perfumed nattily dressed woman tiptoed about the rooms as though she feared she would step into something disgusting. While her husband stood at the head of the stairway, she and the house-mother began herding us children toward the exit. Her husband placed one of his hands behind each boy's shoulders and gave him a nudge toward the stairs. I was last in line, but when he attempted to nudge me, I seethed, "Don't touch me!" I emphasized my wrath by using one of my bare feet to kick him on one of his shins with all the force a bare foot could muster. Thus, my foot served to continue revenge against that man whom I had grown to despise.

# Chapter 2

# INTERLUDE IN PARADISE

As we exited our prison, an additional car besides the one belonging to the social workers awaited us orphans. A large top-heavy black four door sedan mounted upon high solid disc wheels typical of that era had arrived occupied by a pleasant young man and his equally friendly wife. The new lady opened one of the rear doors and invited all of us to enter the back seat area. The social workers conversed briefly with our former warden and they turned their attention to the new arrivals. Within minutes, the two parties separated and we children were delighted to be leaving that dreadful place.

Our charming escorts introduced themselves and their friendliness assured us that we had nothing more to dread. Our long ordeal was over. We traveled for several miles over a narrow paved and winding road through the rural West Virginia countryside before abruptly turning onto a steep unpaved one-lane mountain road. After several minutes, our car emerged from the dense shady forest by which we had been surrounded to reveal one of the Earth's most gorgeous scenes. I, for one, was in awe of a huge rustic log house surrounded by a white picket fence, a lawn with great leafy shade-trees, and centered in an expanse of lush green mountain-top fields. Love at first sight convinced me that I would be willing to live there forever.

As the driver parked the car outside the lawn gate, an elderly man and woman steadying themselves with canes, exited the front door and beckoned us to enter after we had climbed the porch steps. By gesture of introduction, the young woman with whom we had been riding said, "Children, these are my husband's parents. Welcome to our home." The old couple also voiced a warm welcome as they patted each boy upon his head and invited us into a vast living room. There was a pleasant aroma inside which combined that of pine, cedar, hearth-smoke, and cooking spices. A new treat for me waddling her way across the room to greet us was a gentle well-fed gray and white cat. Much to her delight, she immediately became the focus of attention among us boys. We simply could not stop petting her. Alternately, each also boy spent a getting acquainted period upon the laps of our benefactors. They were interested in learning our names and listening to our life stories as each of us also were engrossed in hearing stories about their lives and the history of the beautiful farm.

As the morning passed, the women went into the large kitchen and prepared a wholesome lunch. We children were invited to sit around what would almost qualify in size as a modern corporate board-room table. No doubt, our hosts anticipated that much food would be required to satisfy our hunger, for as you may imagine, we ate with the appetite of starved animals. Our benefactors also ate beside us seeming to be amused and pleased with the rapidity with which we made that food disappear.

After lunch, we were told that we could explore the farm. Freedom was sweet as we ran about the shady sun dappled lawn, the large barn, hen house, animal pens, the vegetable garden, the orchard and the nearby fields. Our lungs filled with the first fresh air we had breathed for months. I personally enjoyed the fragrance of the flowers, tree blossoms, the smell of hay, and the heady odor of the animal areas. I thrilled to the feel of soft grass beneath my unshod feet and the squish of soft damp soil of the tilled fields between my toes. I loved the songs of birds that blended with the calls of the chickens and farm animals.

Following supper, our young female host filled a large galvanized wash tub with warm sudsy water and bathed each boy before we retired to the living room with its warm glow of kerosene lamps to be told bedtime stories. It felt wonderful to be clean again and dressed in freshly laundered clothing, the origin of which we did not know. The next morning following breakfast, each boy in turn sat atop a high kitchen stool with a bath towel positioned about our shoulders, and our sweet young host gave each of us a boy type haircut. It was so thrilling to be treated once more in the manner of civilized humans. Each boy did his best to show gratitude by carrying in fire wood, water, helping to mop the kitchen floor, assist with feeding the chickens, hogs, and the cow. We also each competed to be the one to ring the dinner bell at noon.

Earlier, I related how I enjoyed playing in the dirt under Uncle John's front porch where I pretended to perform massive engineering feats using bricks and blocks of wood as imaginary trucks and equipment. One of the major fascinations for me at the farm was a crude sprocket chain driven but inoperable truck parked near the barn yard beneath a massive shade tree. I spent part of each day pretending that I was driving that truck endless miles while providing the sound effects of a struggling engine by fluttering my tongue between my lips.

I had a deep fear that my stay at the farm would end and once more I would be cast into an uncertain fate. That event came suddenly one day near noon. We children were excited, because our hosts announced that we would be served our lunch picnic fashion on a table located beneath a back yard tree near the kitchen exit. None of us had ever had a picnic. Suddenly a chauffer-driven sedan arrived. We children rushed to see the new arrivals. A lovely young lady exited the car, greeted us, and knocked upon the front door. After she entered, we boys returned to help prepare the picnic table for our feast. Presently, the lady accompanied by our hosts, came to our location. The new arrival was introduced as Mrs. Smith and stated that she had come to see me. Mrs. Smith called my name and asked me if I would walk with her to sit beneath one of the shade trees located on the front lawn. I was surprised that she already knew who I was.

She had taken my hand as she led me to spot beneath a tree. After asking me to sit upon the ground, now holding both of my hands, she also sat before me in order that she could talk to me at my own eye-level. The pleasant lady told me her name was Linda Smith. Without revealing the source of her information, she said that she had been told that I was hoping to find a good home. She said that she and her husband did not have children, but her heart truly ached to be the mother of a little boy. Her home was on a small farm with a cow, two horses, hogs, chickens, rabbits, and Ross, an Airedale dog. The family consisted of her, Don her husband, and her elderly mother.

Petite Linda was young and gorgeous in every way including her gentle voice, the clarity of her faintly pinkish skin, blond hair, sparkling teeth, perfect nose and mouth, and blue eyes so bright they appeared to mirror everything upon which she gazed.

Linda's eyes pleaded for me to share her home and become her son. She said that she knew that for me to make such a decision without prior warning was asking much after all of the disappointments which I had experienced. Based again upon knowledge of my past which must have been provided her, she told me that ever returning to my family appeared to be a remote probability. Although I told her that I would gladly stay at my hosts' farm forever, she informed me that being there was only an interlude; that, if I refused her offer, I would eventually be forced to go somewhere else. Then with emotion welling into her eyes she said, "Edward, I want you and I need you."

As I looked steadily into her pleading eyes, I sensed that I was looking at the face of an honest, sincere woman. Although I wanted so much to be reunited with Uncle John and my cousins whom I may never see again, I felt the urgency to break the pattern of my former abuse. I knew that I also needed Linda as much as she needed me.

Linda said, "I do not want you to rush to a decision. I will leave you alone to think about what I have said. I will rejoin the others at the picnic table. When you are ready, you also return there and I will be waiting."

I sat where I was for perhaps twenty minutes with mixed emotions surging through my mind. I immediately liked Linda and decided that it was in both of our best interests that I accept her proposal.

I joined my little friends who were patiently waiting me around the table. It was obvious to me that they had assumed what transpired. Their excitement about enjoying our first picnic was muted by the probability separation from each other was eminent. Parting from the only friends each of us knew brought back the sad memories of being taken away from our respective families. Now, we would never see each other again.

After finishing our mirthless lunch, Linda and the other adults came from the house. All of us boys stood about with our hands inserted into our pants pockets, our heads lowered in deep thought. Each wanted to speak words which could not be uttered, but actions such as a pat upon my back or a arm around my shoulder spoke volumes.

Linda came within reach of me and said quietly, "Edward, I must leave now. Have you decided if you want to go home with me?"

I sobbed a tearful goodbye to my friends and crashed into Linda's embrace shouting, "Yes! Yes! Yes!"

She swept me off my feet as all of the others, including our hosts, applauded. Linda said, "Come, Edward, lets go home."

After a round of hugs and goodbyes, Linda and I joined the chauffeur and departed.

# Chapter 3

# LINDA, DON, AND GRANNY

The car soon left the farm and entered the paved road at the foot of the mountain. I have no idea how far we traveled or to what West Virginia town. Linda and I sat on the back seat becoming acquainted. I do recall that we traveled until late afternoon before we arrived at a railroad depot. Linda dismissed the chauffeur and she purchased two tickets for an inter-urban trolley. Having never traveled, I have no idea of the depots location or in which direction we went. As is true of many West Virginia railroads, the tracks followed a narrow stony river. We traveled approximately thirty minutes when the trolley stopped at a rural boarding location to allow us to debark. At a distance of approximately a half mile on the opposite shore and serviced by a sandy dirt road was a small village. The narrow road crossed the river via an extremely rocky ford, passed over the railroad tracks beyond the boarding shelter, and disappeared into a dark shady forest. On the seat of a buggy headed into the forest and hitched to a team of gleaming black horses impatiently sat Don Smith. It was obvious that he was not in a friendly mood as he mumbled something such as "its about time!"

With no other greeting to Linda, he growled for me to get into the bed behind the driver's seat. The only other words he said to Linda when beginning the three quarters of a mile trip to the farm house was, "So you brought the brat." He showed his impatience by launching the horses into a brisk trot by slapping them hard across their rumps with the reins. The speed of the wheels passing through the soft forest floor immediately began bombarding me with globules of mud from both sides of the buggy. Linda observed what was happening to me, but Don did not heed her request that he slow the horses to a walk.

Just before exiting the canopy of the forest, I observed the opening of a small coal mine on our right equipped with a loading dock only a few feet above a small rocky creek bed. Linda informed me the mine belonged to Don. Immediately upon exiting the forest, I observed a ram-shackled house left of the road and perched precariously upon a ledge near the top of a huge slate dump. Linda informed me that was where their only neighbors, the Richardson family lived.

The road we traveled turned sharply to the right as we entered a farm field and I could see my future home a half mile distance amid a cluster of shade trees. Don's coarse yell followed by another slap of the reins goaded the horses into a gallop. The dog named Ross ran to meet us. He must have sensed that a stranger was arriving and was leaping to look inside the buggy bed. Don reined the horses into a tight u-turn before the lawn fence followed by a cruel hard pull upon the reins inflicting pain to the horses' tender mouths and forcing them into a skidding stop. The right side wheels rose dangerously off the ground before settling once more with a heavy thud. Only by grasping the back of the buggy seat in panic saved me from being tossed out. Linda immediately berated Don for his premeditated recklessness and obvious resentment of both Linda and I. Thus began my introduction to Don Smith.

In contrast to Don's non-welcome, Ross was straining to reach me as he lunged in an attempt to join me inside the buggy bed. He was so large and energetic, I recoiled from him at first, but I yielded to Linda's assurance that I had nothing to dread from the dog. Once I was standing upon the ground, Ross and I began a lasting friendship. As Linda and I approached the front porch, I saw Linda's mother waving to greet us. Another enduring friendship began with Granny, an old-fashioned lady clad in a floor length gray dress, an apron, and a matching gray bonnet upon her head. She embraced both of us and ushered me inside the house.

Just as had been true with my former hosts, I was smothered with affection by both Linda and her mother. Their warm welcome was a tonic to my yearning for normalcy. But after approximately a year of conflicting emotions of love by Linda and Granny contrasting with the reality of raw abuse of each of us by Don belied what could have been the natural tranquility of the Smith farm.

I do not wish to be repetitive of the same events described in detail by the early chapters of my autobiography titled EBBIE. Briefly, Don's forced involvement of Linda in making moonshine whiskey during my approximately one year residence there resulted in their arrest and my being removed from their custody. Once more I inadvertently became a casualty of someone else's actions and was declared a ward of the State, A three year ordeal was imposed upon me at the West Virginia Home For Orphans at Elkins, West Virginia. I, therefore, fast forward to June 8, 1929 when fate removed me and my feet from that environment so much akin to being in prison.

# Chapter 4

# THE MARTIN FARM

Upon departure from the orphanage, I learned that George Cecil Martin and his wife Dainty of Smoot in Greenbrier County had placed an order through Mrs. Smith, a social worker employed by West Virginia Rehabilitation Services at Lewisburg, to send them a boy, size and age not specified. Without a birth certificate, I had no idea of my birthday or how old I was. I arrived with Mrs. Smith and her driver at Martins' Little Sewell Mountain farm during early evening darkness and a heavy rain storm on June 8, 1929. When their car could no longer negotiate the sodden mud roads the eight miles from US 60 at Sam Black Church, Mrs. Smith and her driver abandoned the vehicle at the Andrews Farm located at the foot of a mountain below the Martin farm. With assistance by a member of the Andrews family, we were directed to a steep path leading for a half mile through a dripping forest, then across a broad meadow of tall grass to arrive at the Martin's house. Once more, my bare feet bore me upon strange ground with which I was to become intimately acquainted throughout the next thirteen years.

As we stepped upon the back porch, through a screen door we saw the Martin family seated around their dining table. They were eating their evening meal. Until Mrs. Smith knocked upon the door facing, they were not aware of our presence. Lon Martin, the family patriarch, shouted, "Come in!" Once inside, everyone stared at us in bewilderment.

Lon demanded, "What do you want?"

Mrs. Smith quickly introduced each of us and explained her mission. She said, "A member of this family named George Cecil Martin has made a request that the West Virginia State Home for Orphans deliver a boy, size and age not specified, to be provided a foster home at this location. We have brought James Edward Martin for that purpose."

She quickly followed that comment by stating, "Which of you is George Cecil Martin? I must complete the transfer of Edward to your care as quickly as possible. The weather is terrible and we must find our way back to our car at the Andrews farm in the darkness.

Cecil stirred uneasily in his chair without rising and said, "Yeah, I did ask them to send me a boy."

The transfer of my custody to the Martins was uncertain as I stood inside their dining room shivering and dripping a growing pool upon the floor. Cecil stared at me with obvious astonishment. Could that freak be the boy who would perform the arduous tasks of farm labor which he had envisioned? I was certain that he was going to reject me. Mrs. Smith was inspired to complete the transaction immediately, being terrorized by the thought of becoming lost in the darkness of a sodden wilderness plus the negotiation of the nearly impossible roads leading back to civilization. It was only through her mastery of diplomatic sales-ladyship that enabled her to accomplish her mission. As soon as Cecil with total lack of enthusiasm signed the necessary papers, I was left standing among strangers feeling totally abandoned and miserable. I was also left without knowing if or how Mrs. Smith survived. For the answer to that, I had to await her annual visit one year later.

After such an uncertain beginning, I soon became integrated into the Martin family and grew to be fond of the freedom of farm life. My early participation in the family's plans was generally limited to what any minor child could be expected to perform until adequate growth developed the strength and ability to perform more arduous tasks. I learned that the Lon Martin family consisted of he, his wife Charity, sons Russell, Cecil, Eldon, Marvin, and Merl in that order of age. An eighteen year old sister named Pearl had died from natural causes three years before my arrival at the farm. Marvin and Merl were unmarried and lived with their parents. Merl was approximately four years older than I and attended elementary school.

Cecil was a brawny twenty six-year-old at the time of my arrival. He was uneducated and had an acute no-nonsense attitude. He and his wife Dainty lived in a single second story room at Lon's house. During daytime hours, Dainty shared meals and housekeeping chores with Charity. Cecil and Marvin worked on their father's sawmill located at Kiefer, West Virginia. Throughout Cecil's life, his farm was only an adjunct to his timber interests. He and Dainty had a week old son named Harry Maxwell born upon their third wedding anniversary, June 2 1929, six days before my arrival. Max, as he was called, quickly grew to become a wonderful brother whom I and most other people adored.

Unlike Charity, who had raised her own six children and had three grandchildren at the time of my arrival at the farm, had much experience being a parent, Dainty had none, but she grew to become a gentle mother of Max and I. She did not demonstrate much emotion, was calm, and was slow to anger. She was quite the opposite of her husband.

The Martin farm first owned by Lon's father, originally contained approximately five hundred acres, but became much smaller due to out-sales to people who also wished to move into the region. Although not possessing the quaintness of the temporary mountain home where I first met Linda, it was located in a beautiful setting with vistas ranging from a few to approximately twenty miles. All of its tillable soil lay atop a plateau with steep forest land extending to the bottoms of the mountain on each side.

The torrential rain of the night of my arrival stopped falling during the night. Beginning with my first day on the farm, Cecil began near daylight seeing that I fulfilled his expectations. With a hoe in hand, he escorted barefooted me into his nearby soggy corn field. I was to learn soon that hoeing in muddy soil is not an ideal condition for cultivating corn, but Cecil was not in a mood to allow his new charge miss a minute of productivity.

He asked, "Have you ever hoed corn, Boy?"

"No Sir," I replied.

"Well, I'm going learn you;" he said as he led me into the rain-soaked field. He demonstrated the use of the hoe between two rows of corn seedlings by scraping away the weeds followed by hilling dirt around a few corn plants to support them upright against the force of future wind.

"Now, that is the way you do it. You stay busy, do you hear? I'll be checking on your work after I come home today. You go to the house for lunch when you hear the dinner bell ring. You come right back after you eat. Do you see that hill over yonder? When the sun drops out of sight behind it, you can quit work and go to the house. Dainty will give you chores to do before supper. Now get started."

So began and ended my first day. Once more my feet sank into moist soft soil and they seemed content with their new environment. They were tender, however, having not been toughened by farm life during three years of orphanage life.

They encountered quite a number of new hazards such as sand briers, cockle-burrs, prickly pears, stone bruises, and above all, chestnut burrs.

My arrival at the Martin farm soon coincided with the Great Depression. There was no shortage of the need to walk during that era. If one went anywhere, most of the time, it was done by either walking or by riding a horse. There were a few cars and trucks in the neighborhood, but the scarcity of money with which to buy fuel curtailed their use except from dire necessity. After being restricted to the orphanage grounds for three years, walking for me was almost a luxury, as you shall see as my story progresses, continues to be a great part of my life today. I truly love to walk.

Having arrived at my new home during the warm weather of June, most of my time was spent hoeing the family vegetable garden and the corn field, but I also cut fire wood, operated the well pump, carried the daily water supply into the kitchen for cooking and bathing, gathered cherries from the trees, blackberries, blueberries, raspberries, currents from the fields, fed the chickens and turkeys, gathered the eggs from the nests, feed all of the animals, milked two cows and helped Dainty wash dishes, churn butter, and mop the floors. On Saturdays, I walked the two miles to Crag toting eggs, butter, and chickens to barter for provisions at foster Uncle Orphy Puckett's country store.

As you can see, I also kept my feet quite busy, but what I enjoyed the most was following the mountain paths to reach the lower extremities of the farm to return the milking cows to the barn mornings and evenings. On those trips, I was always accompanied by my herd dog and best friend Lady while I used a length of stiff wire to roll a round light-weight hoop made of steel. There also were many times when we two friends would race down the mountainside through the dense woods where I would jump as high as possible, grasp young saplings, and ride them to the ground. Numerous grape vines also grew in the forest. I used my pocket knife to sever some of them in order to create a grapevine swing. It was an exhilarating thrill to grasp one of them, back-step up the slope as far as the vine's limit, lift my feet, and soar down the mountainside many feet above the surface.

One afternoon when riding saplings downhill, Lady was running ahead of me as usual. Just as I turned loose of one sapling, with my feet returning to the surface, and I plunging head first and off-balance down the slope, Lady seized a long blacksnake with her mouth. She was shaking it violently from side to side in the process of ripping it apart. The repugnant remains tore loose from her grasp, became airborne, and wrapped around my on-rushing neck. I instantly had a queasy feeling in my stomach at the thought of that mess touching my skin. Fortunately, there was a small stream near the base of the mountain where I thoroughly washed my face, neck, and shirt. Following that, I had a good laugh thinking how ridiculous that incident was.

I truly enjoyed summertime on the farm, especially the planting and harvest seasons. Since we and our neighbors farmed by using primitive hand tools and horse drawn implements, much time was required to accomplish the necessary tasks within the optimum weather windows. As in most endeavors, more can be done with help than working alone. Much of the farming responsibility depended upon me as I grew older. Thus, it became necessary for me to cooperate with our neighbors and them with me to grow and safely preserve our crops.

I fully enjoyed the harvest season when the entire neighborhood of men, women, and children swarmed over the grain and hay fields. We worked, sang, joked, and laughed together as we fondly fostered a sense of becoming one large family. Only adult men could perform some of the tasks such as cutting corn with a hand-held blade to gather repeated heavy arms full to create a bound upright corn shock, operating the horse-drawn mowing machine and buggy rake, or passing pitchforks full of heavy hay upward to build hay stacks. Women and children old enough to do so followed behind the buggy rake as it created windrows. With pitchforks in hand, they gathered hay and piled it approximately seven feet high to make hay shocks. The older children used a harnessed horse and a long thin chain or a length of heavy rope to loop across the shock's rear bottom, hitched it to the horse, stood upon the exposed portion of the chain at the rear of the hay shock to prevent it from slipping off, put the horse in motion, and thus skidded the shock to where the hay stack was being built. Such a ride was pure pleasure for a farm kid.

I was too small to pass the heavy forks of hay to the stack increasing in height with each additional hay shock, but I was just right to stand upon the pile to tamp the hay and to spread it to create an artistically sloped and pointed haystack with an anchoring pole protruding though the top. I puffed with pride upon being complemented as the best stack builder in our community. When I finished topping a stack, I always had the thrill of sliding off its side and being caught by two adult men, thus saving me from crashing to the ground.

Most of we neighbors also grew oats, wheat, and buckwheat, all of which had to be harvested by men swinging a cradle. That was an implement containing a large slightly curved knife-like blade more than three feet in length securely attached perpendicularly to one end of a curved five foot long wooden handle. In addition to the blade, six seasoned and polished curved wooden fingers the length of and corresponding to the curve of the blade were firmly and horizontally embedded through the wooden handle. Each was separated approximately four inches apart and mounted above the blade.

Usually one to four men equipped with cradles would begin at one corner of a field. The first man would begin mowing the grain with rhythmic swings of his cradle, mowing many plants upon the fingers, and then allowing the straw to slide off at the completion of his swing thus, depositing them in a neat windrow upon the ground. Each man moved one step at a time repeating his graceful swing of the cradle each time. Following at a safe distance behind the one before him, each of the other men in turn would perform the action of the first as they moved in unison across the field. That work was fatiguing. Thus, prior to the introduction of mechanized reapers, entire fields were harvested.

Allowing enough time for the sun to thoroughly dry the straw, women and children would follow the windrows and, using handmade wooden rakes, with long teeth, would gather each windrow into individual loose piles. Those raking would be followed by the older children who would grasp approximately one dozen straws to bind the bundles to create sheaves. Other men and youths would follow the binders, stack a dozen sheaves together, bend two sheaves in half across a knee, and form a roof by placing them firmly crosswise atop each shock. Those shocks were allowed to remain upon the field only until the entire crop could be moved into dry shelter to await the arrival of a threshing machine.

Another example of neighborly cooperation occurred as the threshing machine would visit each farm. The machine's owner would earn his fee by earning a free meal and taking an agreed percentage paid in grain for separating the grain from the straw. The farmers' wives would team with others to prepare the meals, which by definition were banquets to remember for a lifetime. We children loved to watch the threshing machine operate as it was powered by the drive belt connected to the same primitive tractor which towed it to the threshing site. The thresher was well suited to its task as it not only separated the grain from the straw, but it boogied and trembled throughout its every component resembling some ugly prehistoric dinosaur as it spit out straw, chaff, and dust.

Most of our harvest days were finished by the arrival of Labor Day after which the nine month school term arrived. Preceding school starting date each of many years, a package from Montgomery Ward containing my school wardrobe was delivered by parcel post. It contained two denim shirts, two pairs of drop-seat winter-weight long underwear, two pairs of heavy wool socks, two pairs of bibbed overalls, a winter cap, a pair of gloves, a wool jacket, and a pair of leather boots. Not only was I going to school for the first time during 1929 with strange students and a strange teacher, my new clothing caused me to smell like a department store and rustled when I walked. I joined Merl in a losing race each morning as we descended the mountain path upon which I had arrived at the farm, now en route to the one-room Anderson School.

Since Cecil and Dainty had bought and moved onto a farm adjoining Lon's, I began the 1930 school year walking three quarters of a mile to the one-room Brown elementary school. It was during the six years I was a student at Brown that many of my most enduring friendships were created. It saddens me that only few remain alive. My memories of two teachers who molded my character, attitudes, tenets, integrity, self-reliance, ambition, work ethic, and patriotism remain among my greatest heroes. One was Dainty's oldest brother, Burnice Haynes. He earned a Master Degree in Education from Marshall University. He had suffered with meningitis as an infant, leaving both legs withered. As an adult, his legs became infected necessitating amputation and, although he owned and operated a car, he could walk only by using crutches. His intelligence and courage were an inspiration for me. After teaching two years at Brown, he entered politics. He was succeeded by Lacy Hedges, a career teacher and World War-1 veteran, who never owned a car or a horse. During a teaching career of thirty five years, he walked an accumulation of thousands of miles through all extremes of weather to reach his assigned one-room schools in Greenbrier County, West Virginia.

One unique memory I have of my years attending Brown. There was no class consciousness among the students. I cannot recall there being a single fight, grudge, or show of disrespect among us. Although it is expected that there usually are incidents of discord among siblings within families, the students at Brown were remarkably civil with each other. We shared what we had with those less fortunate and we all were acutely aware that we were financially poor.

Poor, oh yes, but proud. I shall describe a case in point. The 'Great Depression' dispensed its misery throughout most of the 1930s. Hunger riots and soup kitchens were reported as commonplace within cities throughout the Nation. As described earlier, we lived at an intersection of three roads inside that two-story eight room shack of a house which had become our home. One day a representative on the Department of Agriculture stopped by to ask permission to use a vacant room as the combination drop site and distribution point for free U.S. Government emergency food commodities on a monthly basis. My folks agreed to inform our neighbors that the commodities were free for the taking as long as they lasted. We advised all of our neighbors to help themselves, but not a single person, including ourselves, would accept charity. I marvel that rats and mice did not carry us away, because the food drops consisting of cartons of eggs, sides of bacon, cheese, and condiments continued piling up for at least a year without being moved. The distributor finally stopped leaving them. One spring day when I was assisting my mother with spring cleaning, she instructed me to dump them in the forest for wild animals and scavengers to eat.

There was no janitor at Brown School. By agreement among the students, the teacher prepared a schedule followed throughout the school term that each student would act as janitor one week. When the end of the schedule arrived, the rotation began anew. The student assigned would clean the black board, dust the erasers, remove any trash, carry in the winter-time coal, remove the ashes, and lock the door. During the winter months, the assigned student would carry bundles of kindling and sack a of corn cobs from home for starting the fire in the coal-fired Burnside stove. The assigned student was required to arrive before the teacher and other students so as to have the door unlocked and the stove warm so that no person would have to stand outside in the rain, snow, or cold. I loved my friends and I love that old school to this very day.

Although I have included the following in a previous book I have written, I feel emotional when I think of Brown Elementary and its significance to me. I am therefore including it here:

## OUR OLD ONE-ROOM SCHOOL

In legend, those little schools were always
    painted red
But most were weathered gray instead
Bare clap-board sides on wooden frame
Icons of nostalgic country fame
The one-room schools of yore
By school bus replaced to be no more

Solidly built by carpenter's master hand
Efficient yet of simple plan
Foundation strong, gabled roof of tin
Four-sash windows to let the light come in
Sturdy oak comprised the wooden floor
Access by only a single door

A belfry contained the school-house bell
Whose clang class starting time would tell
That sound wafted across farm and glen
Announcing another school day would
    soon begin
From near and far came skipping feet
Through sunshine bright or snow and sleet

The little room was such a classic hall
Behind Teacher's desk the black-board wall
An open-face bookcase in a nearby corner
Atop Teacher's desk a combination
      disciplinary rod and pointer
Anchored to the floor four rows of desks
      and seats
A pot-bellied coal fired Burnside stove for heat

At the back of the room dangled the school
      bell rope
On a wall a row of nails upon which to hang
      our coats
Lard bucket lunch pails atop a shelf
Inverted glass water jug in a steel frame stood
      by itself
Each student took turns to get a sup
Of water from his personal collapsible
      aluminum cup

Our school was named for a family called
      Brown
It was located upon an acre of donated ground
There was also a coal house and two outside
      privies
Many trees for shade and a playground for the
      kiddies
A board fence kept the little ones out of the road
And a field where a farmer using horses
      his hay he mowed

With first steps from Mother's apron strings
    children came
Like small boats launched upon Life's
    uncertain main
To the care of Teacher's hand so firm
Capable of understanding love or discipline stern
Haynes, Hutsenpiller, Frantz, and Hedges to
    name a few
Were early School Masters whom I knew

School days lasted from nine o'clock till four
We learned patriotism, our homes, and
    Country to adore
Along with grammar, history, geography
    and math
And to make our word our bond along Life's path
To respect our neighbors and to honor Law
And to live in harmony with one and all

Our old school has not lost its great mystique
And oh! If those old walls could only speak!
Of children dressed in denim and gingham
    they would tell
And of girls' pigtails dipped into naughty
    boys' ink- wells
Of arithmetic matches and spelling-bees
And of games of hide and seek among the trees

Of baseball games played using broom-sticks
    for bats
The baseball made from yarn unraveled from a
    knit stocking cap

Games of fox and goose in the winter snow
And farmer in the dell in the spring's warm glow
It was the era of The Great Depression's grip
    so hard
There was no playground equipment in the yard

Those walls could recite all of the children's
    names
Reba, Kathryn, Mary, Wanda, J.L., Walter
    and James
Myrtle, Margie, Calvin, Lacy, Jimmy, and Dale
Leroy, Louise, Lonzo, Larry, Lacey, Lovena,
    Charles, who married Gale
Frank, Ronald, Norman, Tommy, George,
    Biddy, Jim, Vivetta
Christine, Punny Gladys, Loretta, Annetta,
    Wanetta
Max, Layton, Herbert, Ardema, and Irmalee
Last of all, those walls would also remember me

One cannot help but wonder where they all
    have gone
Of course some have departed Life's final shore
It is sad that they shall never again be as one
Rushing through that open school-house door
But in memory I can imagine I hear that bell,
    can see the shade so cool
The trees have grown so much larger now that
    surround our cherished old one-room
    school

Upon graduating from Brown, I enrolled at Smoot High School for the fall semester of 1936. Since this book is about my feet, where, when, and how they transported me, it is appropriate that I relate some of my experiences concerning the real estate located between the Little Sewell Mountain Martin Farm and Smoot High School at a distance of approximately six miles by road. Bear in mind, I could have easily walked two miles to Uncle Orphy's country store, where I could have ridden a school bus five miles to Rainelle High School. But oh no! I must, must, must attend Smoot High School, because Dainty's father had founded it, my inconvenience not withstanding, but as you shall learn, I found two of Life's great treasures there.

Let me tell you about my first day at Smoot High. Torrential rain had been falling for three days, cascading water down the mountainside gullies toward the floodplain of Meadow River. The floodplain quickly resembled a lake where the narrow low-gradient river frequently overflowed its banks. Registration for the new school year of 1936 was required of all first-year students without failure the morning following Labor Day. Since Dainty and Cecil had never shown any real interest in my education and that day was no different.

I had never walked to Smoot, but Merl who had already graduated form Smoot High School, had established a direct route through forests, across Meadow River using fallen trees as a bridge, and across farm fields thus reducing the six road miles to four. Attempting to follow his route during the flood was impossible. I, therefore, walked the mud road until reaching the water's edge. After descending the mountain, I arrived at the edge of a neighbor's farm where the flood spanned a half mile of the road bed. For me, the water was armpit deep. I could not swim, so I should have asked the neighbor to take me across the floodplain on horse back. I didn't wish to inconvenience him, so I didn't let him know that I was there. I removed a stabilizing prop from his zigzag rail fence and used it as a walking stick to prevent being washed away. When I arrived at the bridge, the main current became much swifter, but I used the prop to remain upon my feet. I deposited the fence prop upon the bridge to use upon my return trip.

I arrived at the school almost promptly at nine o'clock. Having been soaked by the relentless rain and being muddy to my knees, I resembled some mutated swamp wump. I joined a group of freshmen who were also dripping chocolate colored puddles upon the school house floor and unable to write registration papers without creating blots. Completing registration required no more than forty minutes for me, following which, I returned home by the same route I had taken earlier. I retrieved the fence prop and returned it to my neighbor's fence corner without further incident.

I am pleased to note that the treks to Smoot and back each school day was not always like my first, although there were many reoccurring floods. On normal days for two years, I walked Merl's route accompanied by three high school girls. After they graduated, I made the daily trips alone. During my sophomore year, I met a pretty brown eyed freshman named Betty Jean Martin. She was the first of two great treasures I mentioned earlier. As of this writing during 2009, she and I have been married more than sixty two years.

At this point, I should not avoid stating that my good dog Lady had died, but not before having a litter. I kept one of her pups which I named Rusty. He had become my loyal friend during my school terms at Brown School and subsequently at Smoot High remained faithful. Although he was not permitted to accompany me to school, he would walk with me to a spot of his own choosing where he would wait until I was out of sight before returning home. That was the same spot where he would rendezvous with me each evening regardless of the weather conditions. He would pretend that he was invisible, but when I came near, he would explode into a rush, crash into me, and after hugs and petting, he would make circles around me at sizzling speed before trotting home by my side..

It was at Smoot High School that I was privileged to spend four years under the guidance of my third great hero, Principle Alexander Ryan Thompson. In him I found a continuation of the greatest ideals which Haynes and Hedges had taught me at Brown Elementary. For a youth yearning for guidance and inspiration from a father figure in the wake of my earlier life experiences, he was the consummation of all for which I was searching. I have and always shall cherish my memory of him.

While attending high school, I learned to play guitar and mandolin. I formed a four-man string band to entertain my school mates and at local parties. The most gratifying performances to me were at the home of Mr. George Mitchell, our next door farm neighbor. Both he and his wife were elderly the first time I met them, but in addition, George had suffered paralysis and was bedfast for years before I arrived at the Martin farm. Our music pleased him, so we visited him many times each year. His family positioned his bed adjacent to a large picture window through which he could view a portion of his farmstead including a low bluff forming the dividing line between his and the Martin farms. I had never seen a kite, but I used a picture of one as a guide and made one. Thinking of how exciting it would be for George to watch it, I flew it for the first time from atop the bluff. I spent most of an afternoon flying it where I knew he could see it. I hurried to finish of my chores that evening so after supper, I could take the kite to his house for him to examine. I frequently made kites which I flew for him to observe until I left home after graduating from high school.

During the summers between high school terms, I continued to help operate the farm and, when time allowed, assisted Cecil filling a coal company contract by using axes and six foot cross-cut saws to produce mine timbers from his forest land. Through hard work I eventually became a muscular runt. Shortly following high school graduation, I was drafted into the World War II Army, thus trading myself and my space on the Martin Farm for a star printed upon a cardboard plaque displayed in a front window of our house.

# Chapter 5

# WORLD WAR II

Most able-bodied unmarried men aged eighteen to thirty five were called to duty during the first draft following the bombing of Pearl Harbor. They included many of my closest friends, thus leaving me feeling much alone. By the time my draft notice arrived, I and only one thirty five year old man with whom I was acquainted for miles about remained to respond. Cecil grudgingly delivered me with his log truck to the required gathering at the Greenbrier County Court House, Lewisburg, West Virginia. Three Greyhound bus loads of we draftees were transported to a large gymnasium at Huntington, West Virginia.

That was where my friend, I, and hundreds of other men stood in a large gymnasium shivering in our birthday suits. I had not been so embarrassingly exposed since the Saturday Night baths at the Elkins orphanage. Among hundreds of others shivering like Jell-O, I spent an entire day inside that unheated arena. Near nightfall, I was herded into line for a physical examination. I had never been so thoroughly ogled top side, front side, back side, and bottom side. Tongue boards were stuck into my mouth, flashlights inserted into my ears, my scalp was checked for cooties, a finger probed into my exhaust pipe, my pee-pee was nearly stretched off its mooring, my heirlooms painfully squeezed, and the remainder of my anatomy was extensively thumped and plumped like a heifer at a stock sale. Besides, the examiners were so stern, they looked at me the way a bull looks at a bastard calf.

Finally, a doctor told an orderly that I was fit for induction. He dabbed one of my shoulders with a swab saturated with mercurochrome to indicate that I had passed the examination. He told me to stand in one of the inoculations lines. That was when I witnessed the most harrowing scene of my life to date as I was passed between two rows of card tables covered by white sheets festooned by hundreds of syringes and bottles of vaccine. I approached and was told to straddle a long bench occupied to capacity by naked men. As we slid forward one at a time, corpsmen standing along each side the tables plunged needles into both shoulders of each man at the same time. I can't remember how many shots I was given, but I remember two which packed the wallop of a mule kick. The final torture was a blood-type test administered by laying one's longest finger on a little ceramic block containing a hinge and a little arm containing a sharp tack. The finger was inserted and the man bashed the little arm with his fist, thus obtaining a drop of blood. There must be a better way, because that really hurt. Since I was told that I had passed the examination, I assumed that I was disease free, but I felt queasy about my unprotected naked butt scooting along that bench where hundreds of others had scooted before. That was when I first surmised that we were cannon-fodder and our longevity didn't matter a hoot.

I was amused by the man scooting in front of me. As I had already turned green from fright about the entire proceedings, he was boasting for all to hear that he had previously taken many shots and wasn't the least afraid of them. As stated previously how badly the two last shots hurt, when his were given, he collapsed and fell to the floor at the end of the bench. A corpsman administered his blood-typing while he lay upon the floor before two other corpsmen carried him out of the way.

After missing the call back at home to join the Army with my friends, I hoped I may catch up with them, so upon given the option if I wished to return home for two weeks before final induction or enter immediately, I elected to go at once. While still as naked as a newly hatched jay-bird, my decision was communicated by another large red X painted my shoulder using a swab loaded with mercurochrome. That gave me permission to go to the head of any waiting line of men. I never saw my neighborhood friend again.

Following that stressful day, we were fed an evening meal before boarding a train en route to Cincinnati. Considering myself as being only a greenhorn country hayseed, before entering the train, I was amazed when an army officer placed me in charge of two hundred men and a heavy briefcase containing what he said were our new military records. He told me to form the men into three ranks upon debarking from the train and to march them to the far end on the Grand Central Station where a sergeant would be awaiting us to be loaded onto Army busses en route to Fort Thomas, Kentucky. He made my task sound easy, but I was overwhelmed upon moving the men into that enormous building with high vaulted ceilings. I had never imagined such a large structure. With echoing voices of thousands of people milling about and rushing helter-skelter, my task appeared to be tantamount to finding a needle in a haystack while trying to maintain a formation of men untrained to march not withstanding. While striving to maintain forward progress as a compact group that must have resembled a mob, I eventually met the sergeant. What he saw must have been disgusting to his every fiber of as he coaxed and herded us onto the buses for the short trip across the Ohio River to Fort Thomas.

Any hope that we would soon be asleep upon our wee morning hour arrival at Fort Thomas was dashed. I had always assumed that the Army was an organization of natty looking uniforms, but I was once more disillusioned that they really had an affinity for birth day suits, when we were herded in to another gymnasium and instructed to strip once more to the soles of our feet. There I stood with a multitude of others dressed only with two large mercurochrome red Xs. We were told to march single file past a large bin containing card board boxes. We were also furnished felt-tipped markers, told to place every item of our civilian clothing inside a box, write our home address on the box, seal it with shipping tape, and leave it upon the floor. Upon finishing that, we moved single file past clothing issuing stations until we had been fitted to every item of uniform including towels, wash-cloths, underwear, socks, and a duffle-bag. We were issued toothbrushes, shaving brushes, razors, toothpaste, and shaving cream. After dressing, we were moved to a barracks after passing another issue-point where we drew a steel folding cot, mattress, pillow, mattress cover, two sheets, and two wool blankets.

The price we paid for the items of bedding was that we could not go to bed near daylight until we were instructed how to make a military bed. The aftermath of all of my inoculations, the travel, the process of being issued my military wardrobe, and trying to learn to accept being talked to as though I was a horse, including missing my own bed back home, was I hardly slept before being rudely aroused at five o'clock by the glare of bright lights and the ear-shattering screech of a sergeant's whistle. Hello! Welcome to the Army!

Events happened fast after that introduction. We were loaded upon a train once more and shipped to an embarkation station located at Chalmette Slip, New Orleans where we boarded a ship named the Alagonquin. It was a huge former Great Lakes freighter refitted into a troop transport with four decks above its hull. We were told that there were four thousand troops on board. I know that there were enough that, if we cared to eat, we were served two meals per day and it was wise to join the end of the next chow line after breakfast, if we wished to eat the evening meal.

Due to war-time censorship, we were not informed of our destination, but we surmised that we were going south when we were instructed to return all of our winter clothing. I made the assumption that, due to the massive draft, all State-side training camps were over crowded and that we were destined to train somewhere else. Anchored near us in the middle of the Mississippi River was another equally large troop ship bulging with troops. During the next few days and nights, twenty two ships which included freighters, destroyers, and loaded fuel tankers plus dozens of smaller craft consisting of submarine chasers and PT boats loaded with depth charges comprised our armada.

Awaking upon a folding canvas bunk located above a column of five others before daylight the fourth day, I was wondering why my stomach felt as though it was massaging my spine. I knew that whatever was happening, I didn't want to be there, so using the pipe frame of each of bunk below me as a ladder, I reached the deck. I climbed the stairway to one the open decks and peering through the dim approaching daylight I could see other ships which formed a single line before ours as we were exiting the Mississippi River and entering the open sea. The ship was gently breathing and exhaling the gentle waves to which my stomach was keeping a wallowing rhythm akin the internal motion of a loaded washing machine. It was to get worse. For the record, I didn't attend breakfast that morning, but I did soon add my contribution to the float-sum of the Gulf of Mexico.

Get worse indeed. As the morning passed, all of the ships slowly took their convoy positions. The troop ships were surrounded by freighters positioned approximately a quarter mile distance in all directions. The decks of loaded tankers had only a few inches of freeboard above the water, thus giving them the appearance of sinking. For security purposes, they were widely scattered, lay off almost a mile from the center of the convoy, and with their gray hulls and minimum of super-structures, were difficult to see from our ship even during daylight. The submarine chasers were nowhere in sight as they patrolled several miles around the circumference of our flotilla. The PT boats crisscrossed in and around the areas occupied by the tankers.

The convoy crept along day and night at a boring five knots per hour changing direction in a zigzag pattern every hour in an attempt to confuse the German submarine packs known to patrol the Gulf. Despite all precautions such as the maintaining strict blackouts at night, no smoking of cigarettes upon open decks, no dumping of trash or garbage upon the water, plus the constant sonar patrols, the German u-boats attacked our convoy our first night out sinking one of the tankers. During the next fourteen days and thirteen nights, we came under repeated submarine alerts and attacks. When general alarms sounded summoning deck-gun crews to their positions, woe be unto any recruit unlucky enough to be in a crewmen's path. It gave new meaning to the term flat out.

I couldn't avoid thinking about the irony of we recruits' situation. Here we were never having taken any training, were unarmed, hadn't even marched, there could not possibly be enough life boats to evacuate two percent of us, and many such as myself could not swim. Each, however, was required to have possession of a life jacket at all times. The ultimate irony pertaining to me was that I had never seen an expanse of water larger than a Meadow River flood, had only vague knowledge of the War, and here I was only eleven days away from home in the midst of submarine attacks. Besides all of that, I felt like the poster-boy for bicarbonate in seasick strength.

Our convoy followed the Gulf shoreline until we reached Tampa, Florida. We anchored inside the bay for a day before resuming the voyage to Guantanamo Bay, Cuba. That was when I became aware that we were en route to Panama. Our stay at Cuba lasted a day after which we resumed our trip. The convoy was only a night out of the bay when a German sub blew the steerage from under the other troop ship. Since our ship continued onward, we were not informed about the casualties or the extent of the destruction. It was a month later when the uninjured survivors arrived at our Fort Clayton basic training camp near the Pacific side of the Panama Canal. They informed us that the casualties had been heavy and that it required two freighters lashed along each side of the troop carrier to limp it back inside Guantanamo Bay.

Passage through the Panama Canal at any time is an amazing education, but to observe it during war time was surreal. The greatest threat to its security at that time was the possibility of enemy air attacks. Should even one well placed bomb strike a set of the locks, all shipping would have to pass from one ocean to the other around the horn of

South America. In addition of battalions of anti-aircraft guns bristling atop many hilltops, thousands of huge search-lights and barrage balloons were positioned along each side of the canal. A small mountain located a few miles from the Pacific Ocean exit adjacent to Balboa was cut into to accommodate the canal with Pedro Miguel locks sandwiched between. To discourage an enemy plane from passing through the cut and destroying the locks, the ends of a huge net, the type used to protect harbors from submarine intrusion, was anchored into the earth atop each side of the cut and stretched above the locks just high enough to clear the masts of the tallest ships.

After playing dodge-ball with the German u-boats, the Alagonquin docked at Balboa with all hands safe. We recruits were bussed to beautiful sprawling Fort Clayton to receive sixteen weeks of basic training. My assigned platoon under the tender loving hand of Staff Sergeant Click was quartered on the second floor of a modern barracks with large glass-free window openings. Click was an arrogant, stocky, no-nonsense Plains Indian with a thick chest, was barely five feet tall and weighed approximately one hundred eighty pounds. His erect stature gave him the appearance of almost being square. He exuded the attitude, "I take no prisoners." With one corporal as his assistant, Click taught us every aspect of our training.

Upon graduating from basic, our platoon was transferred to nearby Fort Amador, a true Garden of Eden on the outskirts of Balboa. We were assigned to the 132nd Anti-aircraft Artillery Battalion for advanced training. I was enchanted by my new home, but had some early misgivings when I learned my new First Sergeants last name was Poison. Unlike Click, he actually was a kind gentle person. To fast forward, he was my First Sergeant at every other unit to which I was assigned through the end of World War II.

Advanced training was a educational experience without any of the unpleasant aspects of basic training. One of the most interesting assignments during my unit's brief stay at Fort Amador was a two-week assignment to one of the anti-aircraft gun positions atop one of the mountains directly above the Pedro Miguel Locks where I could see large ships proceeding through them any time day or night.

Upon completing advanced training, my Battery was transferred to South America to occupy early warning stations for the defense of the Canal. Initially, the Battery was divided into three detachments. The Headquarters Detachment was dropped off at the Galapagos Islands six hundred miles west of Ecuador in the Pacific Ocean; Detachment B of which I was a part went to Salinas, Ecuador; and Detachment C was located at Talara, Peru.

To accommodate the warning stations' needs, the Merchant Marines allocated a decrepit tramp freighter named the USS Johnson to visit the detachments once monthly to bring supplies. Two of its holds had been  retrofitted provide enough tiers of bunks to house a few hundred troops and the mess galley was enlarged to feed them. The Johnson operated within that zone without an escort since no enemy craft of any kind had ever been reported to attempt an attack. The warning stations on the Pacific side of the canal zone extending from Nicaragua on the north to Peru on the south were established as a precaution in the event that the Japanese succeeded in expanding their operations that far.

With the slow speed of the Johnson, it required three days to arrive at the Galapagos Islands. The Navy Seabees had constructed a small port facility at the only inlet along the shoreline of Little Seymore Island, also the location of the small Army camp and Air Corps runway to accommodate B-24 bombers and P-39 fighter planes. The Navy base was primarily utilized to service and refuel daily arrivals and departures of PBM flying-boat bombers, which were on daily submarine patrol between the Panama Canal, Salinas Ecuador, and the Galapagos Islands.

The Johnson remained in harbor only long enough to unload the Headquarters Detachment before resuming the voyage six hundred miles to Salinas. During the night of February 13, 1943, the equatorial temperature inside the troop quarters was so oppressive I could not sleep. Near midnight, I went up to the main deck for fresh air. The ocean throughout that region almost never experiences surface turbulence. In fact, it remains under a calm weather system referred to as an equatorial high. The result is the ocean is almost mirror smooth at all times. Near the time the ship's bell signaled two o'clock, strange events caused the ocean to appear to be boiling as every imaginable species of sea creatures began violently churning the water in every direction as far as I could see in the bright moonlight. The larger fish were shooting above the surface. The flat manta rays, which typically measure ten feet across, were projecting themselves above the water returning to slap their bodies with sharp reports sounding like the firing of an anti-tank gun.

The ship continued its progress as the disturbance caused most of the other soldiers to come on deck. We were growing close to Salinas during first light when we could see small sailboats of native night fishermen. They were cupping their hands and yelling in Spanish, but with the ship's ballast having been dumped to avoid going aground in the shallow harbor of Salinas, the Johnson was riding so high the voices could not carry distinctly. The captain, however, announced upon the loud-speaker that a strong earthquake had struck Ecuador and that a tidal wave was feared would strike. He advised that with the Salinas peninsula rising ten feet or less above sea level before reaching the foot of the Andes Mountains seventeen miles away, everything, including our ship, would be destroyed. Every man donned life jackets and hoped for the best. To attest that the tidal wave did not come, I'm here today telling you the story.

Although the Johnson had to anchor in the deep water of the outer bay, Detachment B debarked onto a flat barge towed out by a Navy tugboat. Our arrival transpired without further incident. The Army base and airport was firmly constructed, so sustained only slight damage. Salinas, consisting mostly of squalid shacks, on the other hand, was almost leveled, except for a few Government buildings made of mortar.

Detachment B settled into a mundane existence of 'make-work' while waiting for an attack which never came. Although I had never made anything more sophisticated than a chicken coop, some superior must have perceived some deeply hidden talent I supposedly possessed and placed me in charge of twenty two Ecuadorian laborers, with my not knowing a single syllable of the Spanish language not with standing. It was interesting. We did, however, somehow succeed building a mess hall and a rifle range. That exercise fully defined the term 'Army expedient'.

Neither my associates nor I had had any leave time since graduating from basic training. With a genuine leap of faith, ignorance of the language in a foreign country and very little money being a major factor, three of us took a three day pass, bought plane tickets to fly ninety miles to Guayaquil, Ecuador's only major harbor and second largest city. Another dumb thing, I bought only a one-way ticket, because having never been footloose outside West Virginia, I wanted the adventure of returning to Salinas through the Andes Mountains by train. O-my-gosh!

The plane ride was my first and it was fine. The taxi ride from the jungle air strip, however, was with a suicidal driver that made me contemplate writing my will if fortunate enough to survive. There was concern if there was going to be ample time alive to write it. Our stay at the Roxy Hotel with its gala evening entertainment was memorable. Being soldiers, we were mobbed by platoons of young shoe-shine boys every time we exited our hotel. They had a most capitalistic inspiration for success and were such a nuisance, we had to get the police to shoo them away. We saw many beautiful buildings, monuments, and fountains. The entire city was enhanced by the merry beeping of car horns day and night as the wild eyed drivers and pedestrians played intersection roulette at every street corner. After my experiences aboard the Alagonquin and the Johnson, I cannot imagine my fascination with my visit to the harbor. My friends had to tug me away from it in order that we could take a sight-seeing taxi ride, which was somewhat inhibited because of extensive earthquake damage. We were fortunate that our hotel manager summonsed a skilled and sane taxi driver whom we utilized only while touring the countryside.

My friends and I parted before daylight the morning of our third day as they returned to the airport and I walked to the nearby railroad station. I was unimpressed by the station which did not consist of a building, but rather an open sided thatched roof supported by poles. There was no physical ticked counter, but rather a man strolling among the passengers collecting fares and stuffing the money into his pocket. Making use of a pocket sized Spanish phrase book provided by the army, I told him, "Yo dissao uno passe por Salinas." I walked to the boarding area and received a shock. Those were the flimsiest railroad rails I had seen. They also swayed as though they had been laid following a snake. I was standing in pouring rain when I received another shock. Expecting to see the arrival of a steam driven train, I stared in disbelieve when an ancient yellow school bus mounted upon the railroad track appeared out of the fog. I looked back at the station manager with disbelief. He grinned and with a wave of one hand gestured "por Salinas." I had sought adventure, but I began to wish I had returned to base aboard that plane. Here I was in a 'third world country' before anyone knew there was one, the region had recently experienced a devastating earthquake, I was financially broke, and could not speak the language.

The travelers did very little talking to each other and did not seem overjoyed to be making that trip. I had noticed several crates of poultry, vegetables, and pigs resting upon the ground. I soon discovered that the last third of the bus was reserved to haul them. I had seen a tall native carrying a long-tailed and unfriendly monkey upon his shoulders. In my hesitation getting aboard that bus, I got the last remaining empty seat near the rear of the bus. My seat mate was a squat native woman with what smelled like a badly spoiled papoose. Fortunately for me she sat by an open window. The man with the monkey was seated behind me but directly in front of a pig crate. The instant I sat, the monkey placed his front feet upon my shoulders, crooked his neck so as to look directly into my face and grinned with his ugly yellow teeth. I slapped him, but when he withdrew, he snatched my uniform cap off my head and retreated upon the pig crate. He jammed my cap upon his head bending his ears down in a Barny Fife fashion while his master struggled with him attempting to retrieve it. The monkey retaliated by stuffing it into the pig crate. The native daintily fished it out, but it was soiled and dripping with filth. I snatched it from his hand, but was not about to place it upon my head. I stuffed it into a pair of my dirty socks and stowed it in my satchel.

As the bus began to move along those wavy tracks, I began feeling a return of seasickness I had experienced crossing the Caribbean Sea. I felt as though I was riding inside a washing machine, I had observed a native lying beside boxes of sand mounted on each of the running boards and facing rearward on the exterior of the bus. Each box contained what appeared to be a sugar scoop. I was curious about their purpose, but I soon learned their purpose when the bus began to travel. I soon discovered that our West Virginia Mountains are mere pimples compared to the Andes. With the first down hill tilt, the natives riding the running boards frantically began ladling sand upon the rails to increase traction. The same applied to upgrades. During numerous repetitions of those scenes with the piercing high-pitch scream of those skidding wheels, I wished that I was any other place on earth. Why was I ever so foolish as to yearn for adventure? I was riding a tiger's back. I didn't want to ride, but I couldn't get off. As that bus careened down those slopes, I realized why nobody was smiling or talking. I was really impressed about our questionable chance of survival when I saw women counting the beads of their rosaries. I found myself almost praying out loud when I also remembered that scary trip two days earlier from the airport to our hotel with that maniac cab driver. I also began to understand why papooses smelled so bad. I took hope from the fact that most of the passengers were much older than I and must have taken that trip many times. I surmised that the reason they were not speaking to each other was because they were in deep meditation with their Maker. Even the monkey had stopped trying to pick cooties from my scalp.

Along the seventy miles from Guayaquil to Lieberatad, sixteen miles from Salinas, there were many steep inclines. Feeling as a person playing Russian roulette at the top of each one, I helplessly accepted my destiny trusting whatever providence which had protected me thus far. The frantic action of that three-man crew was repeated at the top of each one, but hills go both ways. The ones which we had to climb often were as steep as the ones we had descended. The bus crept at a crawl on most of them, but sometimes the wheels spun to a complete stop. At those times, a device attached to the rear of the bus could be remotely activated from the driver's position preventing the bus from running backward out of control. The thought of that happening caused my adenoids to ache. When stalls happened, the male passengers would dismount and push until forward progress resumed. We didn't have to sprint to catch up and remount. What I did not see was any pig or monkey power being used.

The pleasant adventure I hoped to experience came during more relaxing moments when I viewed the magnificent scenery and many quaint jungle villages where passengers got off and others boarded. At one such station, the man with the monkey departed; at another the woman sharing my seat also left. More passengers and animals including other freight were loaded. Since the railroad consisted of only a single track, it was at those stations where side-tracks existed, thus avoiding head-on collisions. It was also at those locations I saw clones of the bus I had been riding. I marveled that there was more than one like it. What a market that country could have been for discarded street cars from more developed nations.

Stops at those village stations usually lasted approximately ten minutes. The rain had stopped and, with the arrival of tropical sunshine, the departure of the monkey and the fragrant papoose, my mood improved considerably.

Without allowing myself to become foolhardy I began to think that I was getting the hang that train-bus riding.

My optimism was short lived, however, for it was not long after leaving the last pig stop before arriving at Lieberatad the bus arrived at the top of longest straight drop I had seen during the trip; the road ran straight for approximately two miles. It had a steep beginning and gradually leveled at the bottom resembling a ski jump. I felt prayers creeping back into my mentality, but the huge gulp competing with words in my throat prevented me from speaking aloud. The bus took off like a rocket sled. The wheels were screaming so loudly, I had to plug my ears with my fingers. I was sitting by the window now and could plainly see the 'sand Indian' in action on my side of the bus. The air movement was so fast every scoop of sand he attempted to pour beneath that skidding wheel simply blew away. The bus must have approached sixty miles per hour and the conductor was incapable of slowing its progress. I felt the urge to also smell bad when at an approximately of one mile, I saw five cattle standing astride the railroad track! It was obvious the conductor was scared. The bus was not slowing one bit. By sounding the bus's feeble horn was the only remaining thing he could do. Even that monkey could have made more noise than that horn which sounded like the muffled bellow of a moose. That was one situation which left no doubt of "Where's the beef."

I had visions of becoming a sandwich of chipped beef from the front, pork fricassee from the rear, with me in the middle. I was doomed to become a crash dummy entrapped inside a decrepit trash dumpster on wheels. I had been spent most of my life on a small cattle farm and was able to sense some of their intentions when they are ready to react. Perhaps the screeching wheels first attracted their attention. Cattle have poor ability to focus upon moving objects, especially at a distance. I had my first flicker of hope while we were yet one half mile from creating Hamburger International. The cows turned facing the bus, perked their ears forward, and raised their heads high. Just as the cow catcher mounted upon the front of that bus was about to perform its designed purpose, the cows raised their tails above their backs and galloped off the track. Whew! That was the pause which spells relief.

I do not think it is necessary for me to explain to you the weakened condition of my health upon leaving that bus, but I will do it any way. Also, when I boarded an Army bus at Leibratad, my clothing was wet, disheveled, filthy, and reeking with an assortment of barnyard odors. I was not surprised the other soldiers would not sit near me on the bus. Then there was the Military Police guard at the main gate to the Post at Salinas. He did not try to understand why I was not wearing my uniform cap. He also was not favorably impressed by my rumpled soaked uniform. And where were those Ecuadorian shoe-shine boys when I needed them? To make that story short, that MP wrote me a citation which definitely was not a love letter. I was required to present it to my First Sergeant. My kind leader quickly realized that, after an ordeal such as I had endured, I plainly needed a rest from my ordinary duties, so he assigned me to an entire week of washing pots and pans at the mess hall under the tender care of a most unfriendly mess sergeant.

As pertains to ADVENTURE: Bah humbug!

The Allied Forces in the Pacific Theater were pushing the Japanese toward their homeland and thus requiring fewer far-flung early warning stations necessary for the defense of the Panama Canal, so the personnel at Talara, Peru and Salinas were flown as passengers in Navy PBY patrol bombers to the Galapagos Islands where our entire battery was reunited after only five months on station.

# Chapter 6

# LIFE ON GALAPAGOS

Upon debarking from the Navy PBM bomber, my feet touched the enchanting soil of Galapagos Islands for the first time. I enjoyed the reunion with the other members of the 132nd Artillery after our five month separation. In addition to that, being stationed there was going to add to my treasures of adventure. During my nine months of assignment there, I was to learn that no other location on earth held the mystique of that isolated region thoroughly catalogued by Charles Darwin and later described by Zane Grey in his book, Tales Of Fishing In Virgin Seas.

The islands are owned by Ecuador, who prior to World War II used Little Seymour as a penal colony for political and convicted prisoners. I never have known their real names, but Little Seymour and Big Seymour were the cover names given them by the War Department during World War II to prevent our enemies from learning the location and identity of military units. For the purpose of this story, I shall call them by the only names I know. I do not know how long the United States Government had established the Naval facility and the Army Air Corps airbase there before our arrival, but the prisoners were gone and there was no trace of what was reputed to have been minimal infrastructure for the benefit of the prisoners by the time the 132nd Anti-aircraft Battery, the 150th Infantry, the Air Corps, and the Navy Seabees arrived. Since there was no means of escape, the story told was that the prisoners were simply released to fend for themselves until death. It was interesting that their only natural source of food had to be gleaned from the ocean and by eating sea birds which could be captured without resistance due to their in-place defiance of humans. There is no source of drinkable liquids. In order to solve both problems at the same time, the Government of Ecuador released hundreds of goats who flourished upon the huge cacti and scrub brush present there. Without compassionate concern for the prisoners, it was assumed that they could augment their diets by eating the goats and sate their thirst by drinking goat milk. A possible limited source of liquid may also have been obtained by tapping the huge cacti plants. No doubt the prisoners became experts of goat husbandry for their own welfare.

The prisoners were gone, but I can attest that, without enemies, the goats were at least a ten thousand strong nuisance during my residence on the island. They were a hazard upon the air strip runways, parked vehicles had to be protected from them, they begged for our food in chow-lines, and ate our uniforms, linens, and hygienic supplies. Woe unto us if someone carelessly left a barracks door ajar. Occasionally, we soldiers would return to discover at least two generations of goats lounging upon our bunks, having eaten our towels, shaving cream, tooth-paste, stationery, socks, ties, mom's mailed cookies, in addition to their donating oodles of poop nodules amply distributed upon the floor throughout. It was every soldier and airman's devout thankfulness that they never gained access to the base food supply. Fortunately our water supply was protected inside huge barges supplied by and refilled monthly by the Navy.

Native animals living on the islands were hideous four foot long iguanas and four hundred pound sea-turtles were commonplace. The ocean teamed with hammerhead sharks, hundreds of types of fish including marlin, tuna, herring, pompano, groupers, jacks. and red snappers. There were electric eels, sting rays, huge manta rays, jellyfish and massive sea-lions. Dizzying swarms of fowl included seagulls, terns, boobies, pelicans, and others too numerous for me to list.

Upon consolidation of our assigned Unit, we assumed a more traditional military life with daily exercise, marching formations, bayonet training, daily gun drills, supervised maintenance, and a weekly hike completely around the island with full combat gear. One strange new mutation of our assigned mission by the Panama Defense Command was, in addition to our assigned 40mm anti-aircraft guns, the inheritance of four 155mm coast artillery gun emplacement and four World War I vintage French 75mm canons mounted on wooden wagon wheels, although we were designated as anti-aircraft artillery. No doubt we were the only unit in the US Army equipped to fight on land, sea, and air should the Japanese come visiting. We dutifully accepted that responsibility with hilarity. Of all the improbabilities, I was assigned as Chief of Range Section for the costal guns. Teamed with Sergeant Eades, we created a range chart inside our underground bunker with its view of the ocean to infinity facing north. Using that range data, we discovered that we could destroy any target within our purview with three shots; one deliberately over, one under, and the killer by splitting the distance. The Navy obliged us on our monthly live fire practices by towing a red canvas target one thousand yards behind a tugboat. With our success rate, it took no longer than a few minutes to destroy the target and the guns became training aids once more.

Well, we never had an opportunity to fire our 40mm Boffer anti-aircraft weapons; just clean them following daily practice drills. More to dispel monotony than anything else, we used the relic French 75s to fire at distant targets across the narrow bay between Little Seamour and Big Seamour islands. As is occasionally true, not all artillery shells explode upon impact, so the day following a live fire exercise, our Commander would load us aboard several landing craft and we would practice beach landings on Big Seamore. After beaching our boats and wearing full combat gear, we would climb the treacherous mountain comprised of volcanic ash and cat-claw thorn bushes, locate the duds, and erect caution signs at the site as warning to any future visiter.

Our Unit made one similar beach assault upon Daphne Major Island comprised of a single volcano. It lay eleven miles in front of our coast gun position and rose above the water line approximately 500 feet. We debarked from our landing crafts near 9 o'clock a.m. and reached the summit before noon. The arduous climb upon that almost vertical lava ash surface with the equatorial sun beaming down while we carried complete combat gear was intensified by the attacks of thousands of shore-birds we encountered upon their nests. No bird, goat, insect, iguana, or sea creature living on or near the Galapagos fear or will retreat from man. We were painfully pecked and flogged repeatedly the entire distance climbing to and returning from our objective. What was more, upon arriving at the rim of the volcano, our Commander led us into the crater whose floor is approximately six hundred feet below sea level. The zillions of birds circling inside of that crater made my head swim while the unbearable stench of an equal number of dead birds, skeletons, and guano made my stomach threaten to turn inside out. The descent to the bottom and return consumed most of the day before returning to our boats. I had no experience in actual combat, but I had been in a relentless struggle all day with birds ranging in the size of a pigeon to that of a goose. Several days passed before injuries to my skin recovered.

With much leisure time after morning drills and maintenance on a typical day, we began the afternoon with a one hour siesta following lunch due to the oppressive daily heat in a land where it never rains. Most of our afternoons after siesta were spent writing letters, swimming in the ocean, fishing from the cliffs, pitching horse shoes, and playing volleyball, etc.

Since there is always the possibility of plane crashes at sea, my Unit was provided two open-top fifty-foot long high powered motor launches. One of the launches was always held in reserve in event the other was inoperable. They were berthed at the nearby Navy base where Sergeant Webb, a professional Maine fisherman in civilian life, was charged with their maintenance and operation. One of our main sources of entertainment authorized and joined by our commanding Officer was using one of the launches for afternoon and Sunday fishing trips. During those occasions, we maintained radio contact at all times with personnel on alert status at our headquarters should an emergency occur.

Another way to vary our routine and to also reduce monotony for both the kitchen personnel as well as the field troops was to utilize the weekly fishing trips to stockpile our 'catch' in the base's kitchen freezers. Typically, a field kitchen was moved to a nearby beach each Friday evening for a huge fish fry. After the meal, we often used four small tent poles and a rope to form a boxing ring. Anyone wishing to box would don bulky twelve ounce gloves and enter the ring for a three round friendly match. The Navy and Air Corps personnel were always invited. Some men preferred playing beach volleyball. The game which I enjoyed the most was playing 'water polo' inside a rope-enclosed court approximately fifty by one hundred fifty feet and played in shoulder deep water of the ocean. The game was played by two opposing teams using a football. No holds were banned and the number of participants was not limited. Any person holding the ball was a tackling target and could be darned near drowned if he stubbornly held to the ball while beneath a pile of tacklers. Any attempt to run with the ball in the water was awkward at the best if not impossible. Advancing toward the goal-line was best done by passing. If you ever engage in that game, you will find it to be hilarious. Those alcohol-free Friday night parties lasted as long as anyone wished to stay.

Christmas Day 1943 was just like all of other sunny days at Little Seymour. Of course we had received presents from home and the mess hall served a traditional Christmas dinner. There is a limited variety of salt tolerant vegetation at Galapagos among which grows a dwarfed most nasty cat-claw thorn bush. Sergeant Eades from Indiana braved scratches to deliver a bit of Christmas tradition and cheer to the troops by cutting one and inserted it into the sand in front of the Battery Headquarters building. He decorated it with small tin cans, bottle tops, and an assortment other trinkets. With that done, he gathered enough softball sized lava stones to outline the shape of a rectangular frame in the sand surrounding the sign bearing our battery insignia to spell Merry Christmas 1943.

Sometime prior to World War II, a group of Norwegian people expressed dissatisfaction with their government by going to Ecuador and obtaining a charter to establish a colony on the southern end of Big Seamore Island. As somewhat of a miracle, that location was the only place among the islands where there was regular rainfall. I mention this for two reasons.  Earlier in this narrative, I wrote that the Navy re-supplied our drinking water by barge once per month. When the US Government made agreement with Ecuador to establish a base at Galapagos, the Navy also entered a contract with the Norwegians to supply our fresh water.  The Navy installed the necessary equipment and excavated the collection ponds for that purpose. They parked one of the huge empty barges at the colony named Academy Bay for a month to be filled, while we emptied a second one at our base.

The second reason I mentioned the colony involved my abiding interest in flying and taking my feet to as many places possible.  I was aware that there were times when flight officers busy with administrative duties often had difficulty fulfilling their required monthly hours of flight.  One afternoon when I was duty-free, I called Air Corps Base Operations to inquire if any pilots were planning to fill flight requirements that afternoon.  The man at base operations stated that I could fill the photographer's seat on an O-47 observation plane if I could be there by 2 o'clock p.m.  I assured him that I would be.

O-47s were referred to as 'flying greenhouses' because except for their aluminum frame, their fuselage surrounding the pilot and aerial photographer was made of Plexiglas. I couldn't have been happier to ride a plane with such an unrestricted view.  I was issued a parachute and boarded the plane with the pilot.  The photographer's position faced backward, which afforded me observation in all directions except directly forward. We flew until darkness just as free as a bird.  The pilot performed many maneuvers, most of which were to amuse me.  He asked me if there was any particular area I wished to visit, so I told him that I wanted to fly over the Norwegian colony located eighty five miles from our

Base. He obliged and we dwelt over the colony at low altitude for approximately thirty minutes. Residents including both adults and children welcomed our visit and waved at us while I was enjoying a memorable experience.

One Sunday when Sergeant Webb was duty free, he invited all who wished to accompany him aboard one of the launches for an exploration of the northern coastline of Big Seymore. In addition to individuals' fishing gear and lunches, the boat's onboard emergency equipment included a great variety of ropes and three pronged barbed hooks used for scaling cliffs. We were many miles from Base when on the horizon at the tip of the island we could see three volcanoes appearing to stand together. Upon closer view, they were almost identical in height of approximately five hundred feet, but one, instead of having an open cone, appeared to have a closed top. Our curiosity compelled us to climb the closed one to investigate. We explored the shoreline in search of a suitable spot to begin our climb until rounding a corner where we surprised and stampeded a colony of sea-lions lounging upon a lovely miniature beach.

For the safety of the boat and our return transportation, Sergeant Webb and two others anchored the boat a few hundred off shore. All who planed to climb the peak began the difficult trek upon a surface much like attempting to climb a mound of wheat or shelled corn. As usual, the steep grade plus the torrid heat made the climb difficult and, as was true while climbing Daphne Major, shore birds made our assault miserable. Anticipating what lay before us, some of the man carried coils of rope, thus enabling those at higher levels to serve as anchors while allowing others to hold on to aid their progress by holding to the uncoiled ropes.

Upon reaching the summit, we walked around the cone to view the other two volcanoes, all of which were separated at their bases by a level surface approximately the size of a baseball field. We were greatly surprised to see that someone had utilized footlocker sized lava stones to outline a rectangle on the sand resembling a modern day billboard. Smaller stones were used to spell 'Fiddler's Incorporated, London, England.' As we stared at the sign with amazement, one the men looked through a hole in the side of the bubble-like cover over the volcano upon which we stood and shouted, "Hey men, look at this!" As many as could find standing room gazed into the endless black interior, but what attracted everyone's attention was a thin metal box resting upon a narrow ledge approximately fifteen feet down the inside wall. Obviously to attract attention, someone had used a pointed sliver of stone to pin a white cloth into the tacky lava above the box.

We could not simply ignore that discovery. If someone else had descended to deposit the box, one of us could also be lowered to obtain it. A rope was fashioned into a britches buoy and, since I was the smallest man among us, I was chosen to be lowered inside. Upon opening the box, we discovered a letter inside explaining the mystery of the sign which we had seen. The letter stated that Fiddler's Incorporated was a financial business and on this occasion during the year 1921 (the year of my birth) the crew of a yacht they owned was engaged in an around the world race. They were also intrigued by the three volcanoes so stopped there to rest. The writer requested that, should anyone find the letter, to use the address to relate how the finder happened to also be there. Once more, Army censorship restrictions forbade us from entering that communication. Each of us did list our names on the reverse side of the letter, dated it, and I returned it to the ledge.

In addition to our Battery, one Company of the 150th Infantry West Virginia National Guard from Ronceverte, Greenbrier County was also stationed on Little Seamore. They had already been there for a year by the time of our arrival. Due to the isolation, the torrid heat, and monotony, it was reported that some of their members had committed suicide by leaping from high cliffs into the ocean. It was rumored that The Inspector General Department had complained about that situation resulting in Eleanor Roosevelt becoming aware of it. She and her female secretary responded by making a visit to investigate. The two women were mingling inside the crowded Base Post Exchange when I entered to make a purchase. I remember how strange it was that among so many voices, at some distance, I could distinctly hear the women talking. Mrs. Roosevelt made certain that she met and shook hands with every service man at the Base.

The war in both the European and Pacific Theaters had begun to favor the Allied Forces, but there remained much to be done. The invasion of Europe was resulting in heavy casualties, so one day, almost without forewarning, a levy was placed upon our Battery to transfer fifty percent of our troops directly to Germany without the men first being granted leave time. The order stated that all personal property was to be abandoned. Only Government issued clothing and equipment could accompany those chosen to go. I have no idea how the choice was made, but I was not selected.

My friend Angelo Sardella was one of those being transferred. His parents were immigrants from Italy before Angelo was born. One of his father's most treasured possessions was his father's button accordion. Papa Sardella who died soon after Angelo was drafted into the Army had taught Angelo to play it. As soon as we graduated from basic training, Angelo had his mother to ship the accordion to him. Angelo helped the men in our Unit dispel many lonely hours by playing music for us. When he received the news that he was going to be forced to abandon his accordion, heartbroken, he brought it to me and begged me not to forsaken it when I would eventually return to the United States. We exchanged addresses and I made a solemn promise that I would honor his request. As it transpired, I eventually brought it home with me on leave before going overseas a second time. To fast forward, I could not reunite with Angelo following the war, because all letters to his address were returned to me marked deceased. Although I cannot play it, I have saved that old accordion at my residence to this day. I revere it as a promise kept.

Within a month after Mrs. Roosevelt's visit, our Battery and the Infantry Company received orders to return to the States. We were replaced by a Battalion of Puerto Ricans armed with 32mm anti-tank guns. Those guns were cute little things mounted on rubber tired wheels and light enough for two men to move them about like shopping carts. We crated all of our equipment and transferred it to Panama's Corazel Ordnance Depot. There was a two week orientation period wherein we briefed our replacements about the operation of the 155mm gun battery, the range section, maintenance, and the ammunition.

One exciting aspect of this orientation and transfer occurred a few days before our departure. In the first place, I could not imagine any sane commander attempting to use those little 32mm popguns to repel a tank attack. It was also incongruous to imagine several dozen of them lined hub to hub upon the beach and pointed out to sea supposedly to sink an invading ship. But that was exactly what was done. I, with a few other fire direction personnel was trucked to the Navy base where we boarded a tug boat pulling a small floating target approximately a half mile behind. The maximum range of those little poppers was perhaps a half mile, so we were only a few hundred yards to sea moving parallel to the beach. I was seated by a table operating a radio when I heard the command to begin firing. I can only surmise that there was a language misunderstanding, but instead of the idiots firing at the target, they opened fire in the direction of the tug boat. Thank Providence that they couldn't have hit the inside of a barn, but men previously riding the boat were abandoning ship in all directions as uncoordinated rounds passed over and also sent waterspouts erupting completely around the boat. I was shouting cease fire. The tug boat personnel were both irate and flabbergasted. I found myself praying, "Feet don't fail me now!" Needless to say, the fire mission was terminated. Up to that time, I thought Puerto Rico was on our side. At that moment, I couldn't care less if the resident goats launched nurdles of goat poop up their noses.

# Chapter 7

# LUZON

The voyage from Panama to New Orleans required only three days and was without German fireworks. Back at Chalmette Slip once more, what remained of my old Unit boarded a train to Camp Buckner North Carolina. We remained three weeks, during which, most of our time was spent making forced marches. One exception to that routine occurred as a result of President Roosevelt's death. The train which returned his body to Washington was scheduled to stop for refueling at Salisbury, North Carolina. An honor guard was directed to be furnished for that occasion. Since most Army posts and their troops were involved in combat training, our Battery awaiting assignment was available. We wore our dress uniforms, were armed with rifles, and were transported by truck convoy to Salisbury. We stood in formation with a present arms salute as the train arrived. The express car bearing his flag draped casket stopped directly a few feet to our front and the sliding door was opened. Presently, the President's valet walked along the depot platform walking the President's little black Scottie dog, named Fala, for exercise. The train resumed its journey in approximately an hour, so our convoy returned us to Camp Buckner.

My Unit was subsequently transferred to Fort Brag within a few days following the Salisbury trip. We were immediately assigned to the newly created 220th Field Artillery Battalion equipped with 240mm Long Tom cannons capable of firing a sixty pound projectile twenty miles. Among the few members of my former Unit remaining with me was First Sergeant

Poison, but all other members of the new unit were strangers to me. A number of them had been trained in armored units, since our huge cannons had to be towed by turret-less tanks. The majority of them had recently graduated from basic training within sight of their new Unit.

Those of us who had just returned from Panama were given a fifteen- day leave. I bought a ticket on a Greyhound bus to visit my relatives at Smoot, West Virginia, but due to the crowds competing for transportation, I had to stand the entire trip. Bless my sturdy feet.

The time at home was far too brief. A flurry of visits with family, Betty, my future wife, and other friends seemed to evaporate. I cut my time by one complete day, because of a sleet and ice storm which further complicated transportation. My foster father, using his log truck, took me to Rainelle before daylight to await the uncertain arrival of a of a local bus en route to Beckley over icy two-lane mountain roads. The driver had installed rear wheel chains which barely enabled him to maintain control. The Greyhound Bus climbing similar mountains from Charleston, West Virginia, arrived an hour late. That exciting trip continued across Flat Top Mountain south of Beckley and Big Walker Mountain south of Bluefield to mention the most major elevations we crossed. That driver was a miracle worker.

A diminutive gray haired lady boarded the bus at Bluefield. She was traveling alone and carried only a small cloth bag. She moved to the rear of the bus as quietly as a cat without conversing with anyone. I observed that she was extremely tense and clutching her bag upon her lap throughout the bus driver's ordeal negotiating the steep sharp curves and slopes of Big Walker Mountain. With it safely behind us, we eventually arrived midway up the last steep grade before entering Hillsville, Virginia. The bus was spinning forward, but sliding backward. Fortunately the shallow right hand side ditch sloped upward toward the top of a hill. The driver was struggling to prevent the bus from veering sideways when the little lady came forward and tapped him upon his shoulder and quietly said, "Sonny, if you will stop the bus, I'd like to get off."

Not wishing to be unkind, the driver responded, "Lady, if I can get this bus stopped, we'll all get off."

Without any damage, the bus came gently to a stop at the foot of the grade. The front of a restaurant was in view at the top of the hill with what must have been the lady's family standing outside waiting for her. All of the passengers exited the bus and walked to the restaurant. The bus driver and I helped the lady safely up the slippery hill. Everyone waited inside the restaurant while a wrecker arrived and towed the bus to the summit. Our continued trip down Fancy Gap Mountain to Mount Airy in decreasing snow was uneventful. Snow and ice soon disappeared from the highway all the way to Fort Bragg.

Training with my new Unit was accelerated and intense. The officer staff and senior sergeants were well experienced in the efficient firing and maintenance of our weaponry. My new duties were assignment to the communications section where we augmented the often unreliable field radios with land-line telephones. A one mil error either in elevation or laterally at the gun location could result in a half mile miss of an intended target over a twenty mile trajectory. Such an error could be fatal to our soldiers, so we strove to avoid any interruptions of communication between the forward observation team and the firing battery.

During early spring 1945, our Unit was ordered to the Philippine island of Luzon. The retreating Japanese forces had taken refuge along the spine of a high mountain range which led southward toward the vicinity of Clark Airbase. Their forces had been divided, so they were following the mountain ridge to reunite with a large headquarters that had established a bunkered last-ditch defense there. The retaking of Manila had just transpired days before our arrival leaving the city in almost complete destruction. Our personnel were loaded into the open cattle cars of a train, which moved at a creep through Manila en route to the village of Alabang in San Fernando Valley. The oppressive odor of death which hung over Manila made breathing almost impossible. Finding firm land suitable to support our heavy guns became an immediate problem within the predominant rice-paddy region of the valley. There was urgency for us to complete our installation and to join other forces trying to expel the Japanese. The natives had suffered unimaginable atrocities at the hands of the enemy. One afternoon a few miles from our location, the starving Japanese came out from the mountains and machine gunned two hundred Philippine rice farmers and their families to death where they worked in their rice paddies. The reality of being in a combat zone came early for us on the very first morning after our arrival when one of my friends standing ten feet in front of me in a chow line was shot through a knee by a Japanese sniper. That same night during the noise of a torrential rain storm, a Japanese infiltrator slipped through our perimeter and killed two of our officers by tossing a grenade into their tent.

The nature of our Unit being so far behind the front lines limited close proximity to the shooting war, thus my actual combat experience was limited. I never had an opportunity to become a hero and I never personally killed another human, although collectively I may have injured enemy personnel through my participation in the fire missions of our canons.

There was one occasion when the mission of my Unit obviously contributed to the destruction of the fortified bunker complex located on a mountaintop above Clark Field that I mentioned earlier. It is almost unheard of that artillerymen have ever gone on combat patrol, but I was chosen to participate with one as part of the security detail protecting our Unit's forward observer and fire direction team which destroyed that bunker system. That resulted in the evacuation and surrender of the Japanese forces on Luzon. The Air Corps bombers and fighter planes had pounded that position for days but could not bring the low-angle penetration needed to destroy the bunkers. Conventional artillery could not be introduced into that rugged area and would not have the necessary throw-weight to accomplish that mission. Our 240mm cannons were the ideal solution without endangering our personnel. The effect of firing our heavy projectiles from such a great distance had the effect of them entering at more horizontally beneath the bunkers, an advantage that bombs dropped from planes could not accomplish The patrol to which I was assigned traveled at night and positioned ourselves at a vantage point near our target. The onslaught was massive and there was no worry about collateral damage in such a remote mountain top. Once the surprise before-daylight barrage began, the Japanese defenders were too busy attempting to survive to mount any type of counter attack. Our withdrawal and return to Base was accomplished with the same suddenness as our attack and we did not have a casualty.

With Luzon pacified, our cannons were stored at an Ordinance Depot and our personnel were moved to Clark

Field in preparation for the invasion of Japan. We had virtually nothing to do as a Unit, so those of us who could not endure being idle found some way to be useful. Realizing the probable need for barbers in combat, I bought a barber kit before boarding ship at San Francisco. I didn't know one thing about cutting hair, but I correctly assumed that soldiers entering combat wouldn't care one twit about the outcome of one of my haircuts. Well, over time, I actually became good at it.

The heroic action of my future Organization, the 11th Airborne Division by parachuting into Batangas and freeing the allied 'Death March' prisoners, brought every one of them to Clark Field to be processed for returning to their homes. One service each of them needed was to get haircuts. Special Services provided tents, set up barbershops inside them, and put dozens of barbers to work on eight hour shifts to provide both haircuts and shaves for them. Those men had been subjected to barbaric cruelty, many of them recently. It was often difficult to use barber tools upon their lacerated scalps and to shave their also lacerated faces. We did the best we could.

Near the time when the last prisoner went home, the season for dengue mosquitoes arrived. The minute pale gray insects swarmed like dust at daybreak with every step troops made. I couldn't breathe without shielding my nose with a handkerchief. Silently during the nights, they would completely coat the inside of our squad tents. I never had malaria, but I was inflicted by dengue fever within three days of being bitten by the mosquitoes. Dengue is called the break bone fever, because every joint of one's body aches. The soles of my feet also felt as though I was walking upon bars of wet soap. I was taken to an emergency ward where

I was delirious for a week. At the beginning, I weighed one hundred eighty pounds. I lost my appetite and weighed one hundred thirty two pounds within ten days. My stomach shrank and I had to force myself to eat. The medics urged me and made arrangements for me to eat five meals a day. Within two weeks, I had a total relapse which was worse than the first attack. To this date sixty four years later I weigh one hundred forty pounds and my stomach has not expanded. If one good thing can be said about dengue fever, it does not result in subsequent attacks as occurs following malaria.

At Clark Field, I could observe the endless waves of B-29 bombers flying toward Japan. I could only imagine the massive desolation they were inflicting upon their targets. We who waited spent much time contemplating the fate that awaited us just any day. I personally felt a jolt to my brain when the news of the drop of the first atomic bomb was broadcast. I could imagine standing at ground zero witnessing the deadly hollow silence as that cloud climbed higher into the sky and suddenly the faint crying of the wounded survivors would become a rending crescendo. And I also cried.

Fate shielded me from becoming a casualty in battle, but having observed the crosses marking the temporary graves of soldiers along every road, the destroyed lives of those who were maimed, observation of the depressing destruction of Manila, and the aftermath of starving homeless thousands caused me to take measure of my worth as a human. As a young man, I had seen the scars of those who experienced the Death March and I asked why? I read about the Crusades of old and I asked why? I thought of the crucifixions by the Romans and I asked why? The First World War was touted as the war to end all wars. World War II was touted to be the one preserving the world for democracy. Neither worked and

I asked why? I have seen the grave stones of Flanders Field and Arlington cemeteries and I ask why? When will man stop man's cruelty to man? Why is the history of man glorified by conflicts to numerous to quantify? Most were justified by some sect or religion. Why should so called glorification of peace and love be depicted as 'Onward Christian Soldiers Marching As To War'? I continue ask why?

A day came when the Army said that I and many others had earned enough points to go home for discharge. Not everyone in my Unit met that qualification, so as we boarded trucks taking us to Manila Harbor, I waved goodbye to them. They were to become the occupation forces in Japan. Should we have remained, either in war or peace that would have been the fate of us all.

The day we boarded a hastily built Liberty ship, which as the Johnson, was a freighter converted to a troop carrier, we began receiving the leading edge of a mammoth typhoon. By the following day after we left port, the full force of it struck us. Before the ballast water had time to fully fill the bilge that puny ship was tossing about like a cork. Every hatch was battened and everything stowed upon the main deck was lashed, and those on deck watch were hooked to the rail by a nylon lanyard to prevent them from being washed overboard. Gone were the days of my seasickness, but here were the ingredients for a refresher course. This book is about my feet which are supposed to point downward when I want to stand, but most of the passage through that storm, I didn't know which end of me was up.

Our progress was uncanny. First the prow would dip below water into a deep trough. The ship would stop and the stern would rise out of the water allowing the screws to beat the open air. The propellers would sound whop! whop! three or more times followed by the ship rushing over the huge roll of water only to ram smack dab into the wall of the next wave in front of it. Millions of the stop and whop sequences repeated until I felt like being inside a washing machine.

We weren't making much headway through the buffeting water, but during the early afternoon of the third day we were in the vicinity of Iwojima, when the emergency horn sounded and the bridge ordered all hands to don lifejackets. The bow watchman had warned the bridge that we were approaching a floating harbor mine dead ahead. The pilot saved the ship from collision by quickly hauling the ship violently to windward  followed by a similar maneuver in the opposite direction, thus missing the mine. The mine must have been one previously installed at the entrance of a Japanese harbor to deter submarines from entering. It must have broken loose during the typhoon and was being rapidly blown to sea. The all clear signal sounded and the Captain issued an audible whew! He followed by the announcing that, had we struck the mine, we would have sank within thirty seconds. Thus, after the cessation of hostilities, we almost became casualties of war.

The voyage and the typhoon continued as the ship skirted the  Aleutian Islands and onward to San Francisco. Somewhere south of Alaska, the typhoon finally blew itself out. New Year Day 1946 is memorable for me for at almost exactly at 12;00 noon our ship passed beneath the Golden Gate Bridge. A barge with a flat top and lashed to a tugboat chartered by the Army USO contained a brass band and a group of Red Cross 'doughnut dollies' was there to greet us. Music was being played and a welcoming crowd was cheering. The doughnut girls were hurling the treats, but the ballast having been drained, the ship was riding too high for them to reach the deck. The sentiment was appreciated, however.

Upon debarkation from the ship, men were separated into groups designated for discharge at military bases nearest their homes. My group were sent to Fort Bragg aboard box cars converted into rolling barracks by vertically mounting two inch pipes floor to ceiling and attaching Army bunks to them four high . The bunk arrangement was positioned along each outside wall with an aisle through the middle. Since it was winter time, our train avoided most of the bad weather by taking a southern route. The trip across the southwest without any major storms was uneventful. Travel by troop train was slow, because freight trains had precedence, so we spent much time waiting on side tracks.

Mid-afternoon one sunny day, our train arrived at a small 'whistle stop' village in Mississippi. As the train was creeping to a stop as an elderly man was walking along the depot platform. He was carrying a basket with a white towel covering it and was calling out in a low voice, "Am sandwiches! Am sandwiches!" We hadn't seen a ham sandwich for months. It was obvious that that old fellow had developed a thriving train- side business with troops returning home from war. Men standing in the doorway of our car actually lifted the man off his feet and deposited him inside surrounded by a crowd. Men were shouting, "Give me one!" Others asked for two or three and so on. I noticed that the man began quickening his stride through the aisle as the basket was rapidly becoming empty. Just at that moment the first customer succeeded tearing open the wax paper which obviously had been sealed by a hot pressing iron. Upon taking his first bite he yelled, "Hey Mack, This is no ham sandwich, it's a jam sandwich!" With the basket now empty, the old man was almost to the other end of the car while shouting, "Yeah man, that's the kinda stuff ya gotta watch." And poof, he was gone.

One night near 9:00 o'clock, our train entered the rail yard of Columbia, South Carolina, A freight train had also entered the yard earlier and parked. We were moving approximately ten miles per hour. Apparently, someone had failed to open a switch for our train to pass through and we slammed into the parked train. I had a bottom bunk near mid-car. I was standing on one leg in the process of going to bed when the collision happened. Every body including myself and every loose item in the car went flying to the front of the car. I landed unhurt upon a pile of men and equipment, but throughout the train were many serious injuries.

When I went outside, I was amazed to see a boxcar resting atop our engine. Other boxcars were a tangled mass of junk strewn upon both sides of the tracks. Fortunately for we who occupied our car, it had remained upright on the track.

By noon the following day, the wreckage had been removed, we survivors were furnished a different locomotive, and we proceeded to Fort Bragg. I was processed through the discharge center and furnished a bus ticket. I had grown to like the Army, so in a moment of patriotic euphoria, I enlisted in the US Army ready reserves before leaving Fort Bragg en route to West Virginia.

I notified my family and Betty Jean, my high school sweetheart and future wife by mail that I had arrived in San Francisco New Year Day and would be home soon. Since neither family had telephones by which I could call for transportation, they were not aware of my arrival from Fort Bragg. I exited the bus at Sam Black Church, West Virginia during a late afternoon, so I walked the eight miles to my home. It was a sentimental experience when I entered a segment of the forest path up the mountain that I used when attending Smoot High School. It had become a bit overgrown from non use, but it was going to become well trodden once more as I would use it to renew courtship with lovely Betty. It felt wonderful when my feet were back upon that familiar ground where they belonged.

Upon reaching the edge of the forest and crossing the zigzag split-rail fence at the corner of a meadow three hundred yards from our house, I prepared myself for an emotional reunion with my dog, my best friend Rusty. Letters from home told me that Rusty had not taken my absence well. Early after my departure, he had spent many days whining and not eating. The fence corner was where he awaited my return from school each day for a vigorous reunion. I hoped that he could hear me now as I shouted his name, so I waited to see if he would come. The sun had set behind a mountain and twilight was settling over the land. I called a few more times, not knowing if he heard me. He had and he appeared coming through the tall grass; not bounding as he did during bygone days, but moving as best he could. He did, however, quicken his steps as I called to him, "Here Rusty! Here Rusty!"

With his tail wagging and looking as if he was smiling, he stiffly lifted his paws to my chest and licked my face and hands. I eased him to the ground where I sat with his noble head on my lap. He had aged. Gone was the gleam in his eyes that looked like brown liquid pools. Now they looked like gray sightless blanks. Also absent was the luster of his beautiful brown and white fur. His eyebrows and the hair bordering his muzzle were gray. To me, he seemed to be a casualty of the war. He seemed unable to snuggle close enough to me and whimpered softly I as petted him. Many of the good times that we had in the past flashed through my mind as my tears splashed down upon his frizzy gray fur. We remained where we were for an hour. Darkness had arrived and I could see lights through the farm house windows. I arose at last and walked to the house with Rusty by my side. I opened the rickety back lawn gate adjacent to the dog house where Rusty was born. He squeezed past me and began barking as if to announce, "Hey everybody! Ed is home!"

# Chapter 8

# WEDDED BLISS WITH BETTY JEAN

Early the morning after spending the first night at my home following discharge from the Army, I dressed in civilian clothing for the first time in almost four years and soon my happy feet were skipping down the mountain path I had trod the previous afternoon. I was hastening to Betty's home six miles away. I truly felt that I was walking on air as I crossed Meadow River upon fallen trees once more and passed through the forests and farm fields familiar to me. I knocked upon her front door near 9:00 AM. I had never seen anyone as beautiful as she opened the door, her brown tresses caressing her shoulders, her soft brown eyes radiating love, and her sparkling teeth framed by her smiling face. A brightly colored gingham dress accented her slender body as she glided with outstretched arms to meet my caress. I know for certain that I had never known such happiness.

After a long moment, she grasped one of my hands and led me through the house to where her mother was working in the kitchen. Mother Mary greeted me and made me feel welcome just as during days gone by. We sat and talked as we tried to relive all that had transpired since the last time we were together. I had very little war experience to relate, having escaped the disaster without a scratch. Betty had helped the war effort by working at Covington, Virginia in a textile factory which made parachute cloth for the Army. Betty's father was at work at a saw-mill at the time of my arrival, but we became reunited when he came home at suppertime.

Late that night, I retraced my steps to the Martin farm. I had reached the mountain path once more on that moonless night and I arrived at a point where a chestnut tree approximately four feet in diameter had lain across the path since my high school days. I had crossed it many times and could have found it with my eyes shut. I would turn and back into a sitting position atop the log followed by moving my feet across to the ground on the opposite side. The leaves of fall were yet quite deep throughout the forest. The weather was cold and frosty that mid-January night, so when I crossed the log in the usual manner, my feet came down upon a ruffled grouse sheltering for the night in the deep leaves next to the log. As you probably know, a grouse accelerates at approximately forty miles per hour from a sitting start. I honestly believe that was the most frightened I have been, when the grouse showered me with leaves combined with the thunderous noise of its departure. My fright was followed shortly by several minutes of hilarious laughter, which brought tears pouring down my face. The experience was not funny enough that I would ever volunteer to have it repeated.

Aside from being reunited with my foster parents, I was pleasantly amazed to observe how my brother Max had matured into a handsome youth of fifteen years. He was a junior at Smoot High School, interested in a business career. He was not familiar with my old foot paths, since a school bus now passed a junction one mile from our home. He traveled by bicycle to the boarding spot where he chained the bicycle to a tree. During later years, the bus route passed our house. Shortly after graduating from high school class of 1948 , Max was drafted into the Army for two years.

I spent much time visiting and entertaining Betty in addition of getting reacquainted with other friends and neighbors. I also visited the families of many childhood schoolmates who perished or were disabled by their wounds during the war. I was also deeply saddened that my dear friends, Mr. and Mrs. George Mitchell, our beloved next door farm neighbors, had died while I was away.

It was time for me to go to work and get on with my life. I applied to Morris Harvey College, Charleston, West Virginia for entrance in the fall semester of 1946. In the interim, Betty and I planned a June wedding. Until that time arrived, Cecil asked me to board at home and to assist him with his mine post business by driving his loaded truck to his mine customer sites. I really liked the hard work, which developed my muscles that had been weakened by the dengue fever.

One of the first actions I took immediately after arriving home was to order a new Plymouth car from the dealership of my foster Uncle Russ. There was a long first-come-first-serve waiting list, since automobile production had completely stopped after 1942. The new car demand was so great, waiting for delivery lasted for months. Betty and I had hoped that we would have possession of our car by our scheduled wedding date. Many weeks passed until the beginning of the fall semester at college was approaching. In desperation, we changed our wedding date to August 12, 1946 in order that we could spend a one week honeymoon at Virginia Beach before moving to Charleston. We were married at Lewisburg, West Virginia, so without a car, we boarded a Greyhound Bus. The war-time transportation crunch had not eased. When we boarded the bus, only two vacant seats remained, but not side by side. Betty obtained a seat near the entrance on the right side. I obtained an aisle seat five rows back beside a loquacious female who began a broadside vocal bombardment of my right ear the instant the bus was placed into motion.

It appeared that was going to be a long boring afternoon and evening trip to Richmond. She halfway squirmed about to face me and, before the bus had barely left the Lewisburg town limits she said, "My you look dressed up. Your suit looks brand new like you have just got married. You have! Did you just get married?" Due to her loud voice, every one on the bus was gawking at me, including the driver who was looking into his mirror.

My face felt as though it was sun-burnt as I was cowering with embarrassment. "If you just got married, where is your bride?" my seatmate inquired.

I blurted out, "She is occupying the front seat."

The other passengers erupted into pandemonium. They began to shuffle the seats so that Betty and I were seated together upon the one opposite where I had been sitting. Everyone began shouting congratulations and a lively party began with most of the passengers telling about their wedding days and how they met their spouses. The bus driver named Buckshot Jones was a comedian who kept the fun going until arriving at Lexington, many passengers exited and new ones boarded. With the arrival of darkness, some of the seats became vacant. It transpired that my former seatmate was then alone. Being the busy-body she obviously was, she leaned her back against the window, curled her legs upon the seat so she was facing us, and she never stopped spying until we left the bus at Richmond to change onto another bound for Virginia Beach.

We rented the honeymoon suite in the former beach front Driftwood Hotel constructed of weathered cypress wood. Following our long bus ride, we spent most of the day sunning on the beach and sightseeing. Following a late evening meal, we retired to our room where, from our balcony we saw the gorgeous full moon rise above the ocean water. While observing the beautiful scene before us, we cuddled in a large lounge chair and talked about how fortunate we were to have survived the war and that we could now resume our lives together. As we planned our future and discussed the children we would share, I felt deep emotions when realizing at last I had become a member of my own family. Now I felt as though I was whole. I belonged. Life among strangers was gone forever and I was married to the girl I loved.

With our honeymoon over, when we dismounted from the bus at Sam Black Church near Betty's home, her brother Willard and his wife Anna Jane from Washington were waiting for us. They took us to Betty's home where her relatives and a good dinner awaited us. Although Willard knew that we had planned to also return to my home and then return, he seemed to delay our departure until almost darkness.

Betty and I were treated to a great surprise when first we could see the farmhouse. There behind the closed driveway gate was a bright new Plymouth sedan! Max had learned that it had arrived at the dealership, so he made arrangements with Uncle Russ to allow him to bring it home for us.

After a round of greetings and welcomes home, of course Betty and I were anxious to examine our new car, but mysteriously, Max would not allow us to have the keys until after refreshments that Dainty and some of the neighbor women prepared were served.

Betty and I 'smelled a rat', having been educated in the customs of country folk following a wedding. I had anticipated some shenanigans might be in store for us, so I had purchased a few boxes of cigars before returning from Virginia Beach. It was customary for a groom to give cigars to all male well wishers. The night air was warm, but I observed that every window of the house was raised for perhaps another purpose. While sipping punch, I drew Betty's attention to some strange shadows moving among the shrubbery surrounding the lawn and I was certain I heard a few clinking sounds. All of the sudden, all creation broke loose completely surrounding the house as bugles, cowbells, pounded dishpans, drums, and anything else which could render noise were used. The noise sounded as though it was indoors. As the men and children marched around the outside, more neighborhood women arrived with more goodies.

As tradition dictated, the bride and groom had to come out into full view and engage in a long embrace until the noise ceased. That was followed by everyone passing and congratulating us newly weds. The men seized me and every one cheered as they rode me astraddle a fence rail. Following that, I passed cigars and the women served everyone refreshments. The party lasted until near midnight when Betty and I followed Willard in our new car back to Betty's home. I felt embarrassed to go to bed with Betty for the first time at her parents home, but her mischievous brother dispelled some of my anxiety when we discovered that he had tied a cow bell to our bed springs! I was certain that Betty's parents were also aware of the prank.

Betty had numerous relatives residing in the Charleston area, including an aunt and uncle who welcomed us to use a spare bedroom until we could hopefully rent an apartment. With so many returning veterans, students, and job seekers pressuring a housing crunch, we obtained a single room and bath from a family of three who had a room to spare. We were fortunate that they also allowed us cooking privileges. We purchased necessary linens, a small radio, and an electric hotplate. We purchased small quantities of food and, during the cold winter months, used an outside window sill as a refrigerator.

Betty did not seek employment immediately. Fortunately, city transportation was available just outside our door, saving me from having to drive our car into the business center and paying parking fees. That left our car available to Betty to shop and spend time with her aunts, uncles, and cousins, who did everything possible to help us begin married life.

Morris Harvey College had been previously located at Barboursville, a suburb of Huntington, West Virginia, where Daintie's father had at one time been a professor of English. For reasons unexplained, it arrived at Charleston without a campus. The result was that it established headquarters on the top floor of the former Charleston Public Library building and leased public school classrooms and at the Masonic Hall. Each was within four city blocks of each other, but the inconvenience was that I and many others had daily classes inside each of them. A standing joke was Morris Harvey students running between classes were the fastest moving objects on earth. I can still envision us with out coattails standing straight out as we ran through traffic to reach classes on time.

Since my only income was that provided by the Veterans GI Bill, I arranged all of my seventeen semester hours of classes during forenoon so I could hold a job in the shipping and receiving department of Sears and Roebuck. That arrangement worked fine throughout 1946 and 1947, but we discovered that Betty had become pregnant. She gave birth to our son, Rodney, at the former Mountain State Hospital on April 29, 1948.

Rodney's arrival began filling our hopes for creating the family I had never known and Betty wanted to share. Our joy was boundless as we carried that little fellow home and began accustoming our selves to being Mom and Dad.

Another aspect of our lives was, with increased needs of both income and living-space, I foresaw that I must drop out of college at the end of that semester to earn enough income to return later to complete a degree. My foster uncle and good friend Orphy Puckett, country merchant and Crag, West Virginia Post Master, informed me that the New River Grocery Company of Hinton, West Virginia was advertising to hire three book keepers to convert their archaic business methods to a cost-accounting system. I hastened to apply in person and was hired as an aide to the Chief Accountant. Betty and I were fortunate to find a small furnished reasonably priced efficiency apartment near my job. I began earning enough to create a saving account and adequate standard of living. I became respected at work and was enjoying my new life. The other employees such as warehousemen, road salesmen, and drivers were mostly elderly men, who had been with the company since its inception. The Company's owner, hoping to provide me with work on a permanent basis, saw a potential future for me. Therefore, my position at Hinton was cut short within the year when the Manager of the company's branch location at Rainelle, West Virginia announced his intention to retire by the end of 1949. President Miller conferred with me and stated that I was being groomed to replace the retiring branch manager, so I was transferred to the branch route sales department to gain experience and acquaintanceship with the merchant customers who kept us in business.

Betty, Rodney, and I immediately returned to the vicinity where we had grown to adulthood. I was fortunate to find a small modern four room house with a full basement on two acres of ground beside the highway within two miles of my new place of employment. The wife of the man who owned the house had recently separated from him, so in his state of sadness, he offered it fully furnished to me for six thousand dollars. I was overwhelmed. We shook hands on the promise that I would go to the Bank of Alderson the next day to negotiate the purchase, providing that he would continue to live there until the purchase was consummated. I hired a photographer to use a Speed graphic camera to produce an eight by ten inch picture of the house. I took it with us when Betty and I went to the bank.

I had never been inside the Alderson Bank before that day, and had also never met any of the bank personnel. I knew that both my foster father and Betty's father had accounts there and knew the Bank President well. I introduced ourselves to him and stated the purpose of our visit. I related to that I was recently discharged from the Army, that we were married, had a son, and that I was employed as a salesman for New River Grocery Company. I told him that I had not established an account with any bank during my brief working career. I told him about the opportunity to purchase the house at a bargain upon which I presented the picture to him. He viewed the picture and agreed that it was an attractive piece of property. He inquired who our parents were and seemed impressed with our answers.

He then asked me how I intended to go about purchasing the house. I told him that we hoped to borrow the entire amount from his bank. He asked me to name three outstanding citizens whom I knew and may get to indorse a deed of trust to secure the loan. I named three people whom he knew well and he prepared the deed of trust. He handed it to me and instructed to return the paper to him, if I succeeded in obtaining the signatures. We shook hands and parted. Two days later, I returned with the required signatures and the loan was consummated. I paid the seller and we moved into our neat little house, our first home.

My new coworkers were introduced to me and the orientation of my new position began. I was warmly received by the Manager and he arranged for me to ride with each of the route salesmen whereby I learned the names and locations of each of our customers. I was given a company car and was assigned the route of a scheduled retiree. The route salesman work schedule was Monday through Friday. My route included all retail country stores inside a circle of approximately thirty miles radius North, East, and South of Rainelle. My customers were some of the kindest, gentlest, and lovable people I have ever known. That seemed to be the normal standard of the folk who owned and operated the combination Post Office/country stores of yore.

Following World War II, there was an ominous ten year period of economic stirring, awakening, and growing competition as highways and rapid transportation encouraged the strong to devour the weak. That caused the demise of New River Grocery Company. Within four months of accepting my new job, I was asked to return to the Hinton Headquarters for a conference where all attendees were informed that a Corporation located at Chicago was proposing to liquidate New River Grocery and all its known competitors in Beckley and Charleston. They offered an attractive buy-out too good to refuse. They sent in a team with whom I was instructed to work helping dismantle our company. Of course, I was facing unemployment once more. The out-going president of New River Grocery was so flattering of me that the Chicago firm offered me a position at their headquarters, but I declined.

Once more my good friend Orphy came to my rescue. He told me that a position as a postal clerk was vacant at the East Rainelle Post Office. Being a post master himself, he recommended me for the position to Post Master Richard Quick. I was hired immediately following a brief back-ground investigation. The pay enabled me to create a savings account, which would support my return to Morris Harvey in time. My work schedule was Monday through noon Saturday and I had to perform a thirty-minute dispatch to a postal train each Sunday morning. Ah! Life was good with Betty and Rodney in our little house. We had everything we needed. I renewed old friendships and made many new ones. In addition, my boss and coworkers were fun to be near.

There was a geological formation within the Meadow River water shed about one mile below Rainelle which, although not a dam, was high enough to cause water to pool and form a flood-plain which encompassed the entire town site. At least one time every winter or spring for many years, snow melt and heavy spring rains would often flood most of Rainelle to a depth of five feet. Those floods occurred many years until the Army Corps of Engineers used high explosives to remove the impedance. Such a flood happened the first winter I worked at the Post Office. It occupied a small one-story building whose floor level was almost exactly that of the street and sidewalk. During one late afternoon, the water began to rise above the postal workers shoe tops. Mr. Quick dismissed all except he and myself. There was a limit to how high we could stack mail and equipment above the rising waters to safeguard it. We began by stacking desks upon tables and chairs upon them. There was always a surplus of the standard mail sacks, so we filled as many of them as needed to hold undelivered mail, records, stamp stock, blank money orders, small office machines, and anything else which the bags could securely enclose and that we could lift. Of course we could not lift the safe, but it could be easily cleaned after the water receded.

We worked until near eight o'clock when the water stopped rising at our armpit level. Our coworkers had evacuated to shelters, for their houses including Mr. Quick's were uninhabitable. Both he and I had taken precaution during the afternoon to position our cars upon high ground, so when he finally locked the Post Office, we waded to them and utilized un-flooded streets to reach my house. We took baths, washed and dried our clothing, ate super, and went to bed. The next morning arrived bright and sunny. We waited until the flood waters slowly subsided and began cleaning the mess it left behind.

One day, a railroad engineer who had been transferred to Rainelle from another town was seeking a house to buy. I was anxious to return to Morris Harvey for the fall semester of 1950. I was sure that, with the money we had saved combined with the stipend provided by the GI Bill, we could survive. After discussing the idea with Betty, we agreed to sell the house without including the furnishings. The engineer agreed to pay us eight thousand dollars cash for it. The buyer accompanied me to the Alderson Bank where he paid off the deed of trust, thus consummating the sale.

Betty and I vacated the house and spent a few days with our folks, postponing resignation from the Post Office until a replacement was found. Thereupon, Betty and I spent a few more days visiting with her Charleston relatives until we succeeded renting a two story five room house just in time to move in and start attending classes.

It is amazing how distant world affairs can unexpectedly involve someone. It was the outbreak of the Korean War which ensnared me. I received my recall to the Army after attending one week of classes at Morris Harvey. I was devastated. It seemed unreal. If I had an inkling that would happen, we could have remained inside our little house at Rainelle and Betty and Rodney would have been only a few miles away from both of our families. Now I had to leave my young wife and a two year old son in a rented house far from home after a few days notice to once more participate in a senseless exercise of man's cruelty to man a half of a world away. I rued the inane inspiration to join the reserves. Considering my circumstances, no doubt I could have appealed for an exemption based upon status as a student as well as being married with a child. I was also facing a financial hardship, because I was returning to the Army with a fifty dollar per month rank of private.

Without waiting to be asked, Betty's parents, Tuck and Mary Martin along with Betty's young sister, Bonnie, closed their house at Smoot and voluntarily came to Charleston to stay with Betty until our situation evolved. As you can imagine, I was in torment of my own making. On August 28, 1950, Betty, Rodney, and I tearfully faced a truly uncertain future as I mounted a train en route to Fort Campbell, Kentucky.

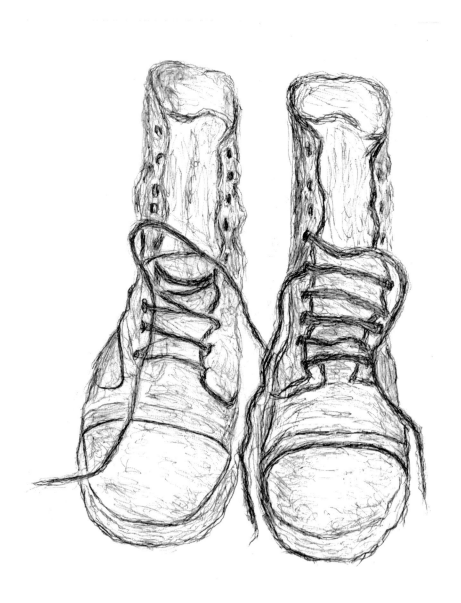

# Chapter 9

# JUMP BOOTS

August 28, 1950 was the date of my deepest despair. I felt as though my heart was being torn from my body as Betty and I embraced while holding Rodney between us for possibly our last time. The train, which would carry me to Fort Campbell, Kentucky, was already moving as we clung to each other. I was emotionally drained and my feet felt like lead as I hurried to get aboard. I looked back from the open doorway until I could no longer see my greatest treasures. I became angry with myself as I rued my inane decision to join the Reserves at Fort Bragg.

Several other recalled men occupied the car I was riding, but there was little conversation among us, as in deep thought, we felt loneliness for the families we had left behind. The train arrived during the late afternoon at what was at that time the sleepy little town of Clarksville, Tennessee. It was, however to experience a massive influx of population and business, due to the arrival of thousands of men and families at Fort Campbell seven miles away. An Army bus took us to Fort Campbell. That Post had been mostly dormant following World War II, but was now being rejuvenated in preparation for basic trainees and reactivated reservists.

We arrivals were temporarily housed at the reception center where we were given physical examinations, inoculations, aptitude tests, and our individual personnel files were created. I had most of my meager pay placed into an allotment for Betty and also made she and Rodney beneficiaries of an insurance policy.

I mentioned in Chapter 7 that the 11th Airborne Division had rescued the Death March prisoners at Batangus. Following that, the Division went to Japan for occupation duty. Shortly prior to the beginning of the Korean War 11th returned to the United States and was stationed at Fort Campbell. I had wanted to become a paratrooper during World War II, but was never at the right place at the right time. Not that I wanted to be in my current situation, but if I had to be, I could not have been more pleased when I was assigned to Battery B, 165th Airborne Field Artillery Battalion for refresher training. In addition, most of the men of Battery B at that time were from West Virginia. That was my opportunity to become a paratrooper, since I had to be there anyway. There was a glitch, however. Being in the Reserves, I was committed to what was termed a 'pipeline' to Korea with no possible deviation.

The entire Division had been reduced in manpower to peace cadre strength and all of its equipment and vehicles were coated with heavy grease and stored inside motor pool buildings. One jeep was allocated the Battery B's commanding officer and one truck was used as needed. Somewhat of a dilemma existed, because every Unit within the Division was going to be in need of personnel to perform training duties. No man could be forced to become a paratrooper, because joining was entirely voluntary. Non-jumpers could belong to the Division, but with troop reduction through out the Army following World War II, filling the ranks was going to take time.

I had made my wishes known to Battery B First Sergeant, who stated that he knew of an obscure provision in Army Regulations which would allow me to break out of the pipeline, if I wished to be discharged from the Reserves and join the

Regular Army. I knew that a three year enlistment was a finite period, whereas service in the pipeline was indefinite at best. So, on December 12, 1950, I became a member of the Regular Army. That did not preclude my going to Korea, but volunteering to go to the Paratroop Training School, Fort Benning, Georgia gave me a reprieve during which I would be more in control of my destiny. Besides, the First Sergeant reserved the position as Battery Clerk for me upon my return and a promotion to Private First Class broke me out of the fifty dollar per month pay grade. Should I successfully graduate from Jump School, I would also earn an additional fifty dollars per month.

I wrote a letter to Betty almost daily and called her when I could afford to. Looking forward to the possibility that I could move her to Clarksville upon graduating from Jump School in January lifted both of our spirits. Paratroop School had a reputation of being difficult and separating the weak from the strong, but the challenge only strengthened my determination to succeed. I had every reason to win.

During the interlude from August through December, I witnessed a problem a Unit experienced by being at cadre strength. Due to the lack of a qualified Mess Sergeant, I ate the worst food I can remember. With no one else to fill the position, the Battery B Motor Sergeant, who didn't know zilch about cooking, held the position. His cooking staff was comprised of his mechanics, members of the communications section, and 'cannon cockers' from the firing battery. What a great day of celebration came when a fully trained Mess Sergeant was assigned to Battery B.

During January, I was enrolled in the first parachute training class of 1951 at Fort Benning. One other member of Battery B accompanied me, but the other approximately two hundred trainees were from military bases throughout the Nation. We were assigned to platoons delineated by the initials of our last names. I was designated Platoon Leader of all whose last names began with J, L, and M. We trained Monday through Saturday with our days starting at 5:00 AM. Reveille and roll call followed a quick visit to the toilet. Immediately thereafter, the school cadre formed each platoon into a column of three and we were treated to a two mile close-order run while shouting cadence to exercise our lungs and keep in step. After returning for breakfast, we performed our personal hygiene, made our beds, and cleaned the barracks. Following that, we 'fell out' in formation for inspection followed each day's training.

The first week was devoted mostly to physical training. All movements, both individual or in formation, were done at a run. Anyone observed walking was assessed twenty pushups or setups. Any other mistake also brought a fine of pushups or pull-ups. Any trainee who fell out of step or began to lag behind was required to run an number of circles around his moving platoon with one arm extended horizontally while shouting "I'm a P-51 with a broken wing." That good natured humor helped ease the tension of the arduous training. If, however, a trainee failed to measure up to the physical standards and consistently fell out of formations for either physical reasons or lack of commitment, he was dropped from the program at the end of the day. Those individuals were transferred to the replacement center to be returned to their home Base before nightfall.

During week two we continued the relentless physical and mental toughness training, but we were then introduced to a series of 'mock-up' training aides such as exiting plane doors, practicing parachute landing falls as we jumped off six foot high platforms, being suspended by parachute harness while practicing directional slipping techniques, and recovering to a standing position from lying flat upon our backs while wearing a parachute and being driven across the ground by the blast from a powerful stationary propeller. The entire last two days were devoted to jumps from thirty two foot high towers. Stairways led up to an enclosure constructed to resemble the interior of a plane. While at ground level, the students put on parachute harnesses. Upon reaching the jump level, the trainee's harness was snapped to a fifteen foot static line, he was instructed to assume the proper pre-jump stance inside the doorway facing outward. The opposite end of the static line was permanently attached to a hooded 'death-slide' pulley through which passed a one inch thick steel cable. The cable, which extended approximately fifty yards, was securely anchored on each end into imbedded power-line poles. After shouting his name and trainee ID number to a grading sergeant standing upon the ground, another sergeant standing behind the jumper, would forcefully tap him on his buttocks and shout, "Go!

The jumper must follow the proper exiting procedure he had been taught him to prevent him from crashing into the retaining pole. Each jumper had to pretend to check his parachute's condition before crossing a stripe of lime upon the ground, and glide on the trolley to a high earthen mound where two men snagged him. Each man had to make five properly executed jumps before he earned a passing grade. Fear of exiting the thirty four foot towers was the greatest cause of jump school failures. That was how I lost only one man from my platoon by his refusal to jump.

Those having passed were marched across the training field where four two hundred foot towers awaited them. They were constructed of steel frameworks. Each tower contained four arms to which a drum of steel cable with pulleys and an electric motor were attached. The cables were lowered to the ground where complete parachutes were affixed. The trainees donned parachutes and were hoisted to the top of their respective tower arms. Each jumper's ride was automatically halted six feet from the top. His individual grader upon the ground communicated via a speaker attached to the arm he was on to inquire, "Are you ready?" If the jumper answered affirmatively, the cable moved to the trip point and the jumper floated to the ground. To make the passing grade, each jumper had to demonstrate directional slips, assume the proper landing attitude before reaching the ground, followed by a perfect parachute landing fall. That phase of training was enjoyable, but most men made certain that they performed properly the first time rather than draw negative attention to themselves.

Week three was jump week. Daybreak seemed to come fast after a week end of deep thinking, apprehension, and sober bravery checks. Morning calisthenics and two mile runs were discontinued. Breakfast was served before daybreak, following which we boarded trucks en route to the Air Force's Lawson Field. We dismounted and were grouped into our established platoons. Each platoon marched single file past parachute issuing tables where each man was given a main parachute and a reserve one. Upon leaving the issuing building, we entered another appropriately called 'the sweat shed.' There were many somber faces there including mine. The same instructors who had supervised us to date were in attendance now to assist us in properly fitting and adjusting the parachutes. We were told that it was imperative that all harness straps be tightened until they became uncomfortable in order to avoid painful abrasions to our shoulders and groins during the parachute's opening shock. I was bound so tightly, I could not stand erect when walking to the plane.

Inside the plane for our initial jump, there was a jumpmaster assigned to each door. The first jump was called an individual tap out identical to the procedure when jumping from the thirty five foot tower. During mock-ups of our second week of ground training, we rehearsed in-plane safety practices enacted immediately before jumping. Now when ordered by the Jumpmaster, we stood up, hooked our static line snap fastener to the overhead anchor cable, counted off from front to rear, made an equipment check of first the front of our own equipment followed by checking that on the back of the jumper standing next in line. If all is well, again from the front of the plane we shouted number one OK, number two Ok, and so forth simultaneously striking a buttock of the next man in front until reaching the Jumpmaster. There upon, Jumpmaster shouted, "Shuffle and stand in the door." All of that transpired while a red light glowed above the exit door. When the plane reached the drop zone, a green light appeared. On ordinary jumps, each trooper is allowed two seconds in the door. Any delays are hazardous to remaining jumpers, who may land in areas beyond the landing zone.

The length of landing zone is generally designated by the number of seconds it takes for the jumpers to exit. Thus, as pertained to the plane we were riding with twenty one men per 'stick' multiplied by two seconds, the drop zone ideally would be a forty two second one. Obviously, engaging in individual tap-outs, the planes would have to make several passes to test jump the entire load.

There were no long faces in the barracks that night. Most of the men were chattering like magpies about their new experience. I was no exception, but by bedtime, I took a reality check. Of course I had made a successful jump while swept up with euphoria, but I must admit that I was more fearful of my second jump that any of the two hundred forty that I eventually made.

The weather throughout our jump week was clear and dry. Beginning with the second day, our jumps were of the standard two seconds in the door variety. None of the men of my platoon refused to jump, so all went well with me also until my fifth and final qualifying jump. The luck of the draw so to speak positioned me as the last man in the right side stick. One or more men ahead of me were slow exiting the door. We were flying toward Phenix City where heavy forest cover and the Chattahoochee River bordered the drop zone. When my parachute opened, I discovered that I had been dropped far off target over the forest. I was almost certain that I would have to make a dangerous tree landing, but I followed my training instructions by climbing my suspension lines almost to the edge of my parachute in a desperate slip toward the drop zone. Slipping at such a steep angle caused my chute to spill air rapidly and to increase the rate of drop. I was making progress toward the drop zone, but I had to lift my feet to avoid a treetop at the edge of the field. The resulting seconds I lost made it impossible to take a proper landing position. I crashed onto the ground with most of my weight on my left leg as I rolled into a tangled package of silk and suspension lines. A sharp pain raced through my left thigh as I lay for a moment to determine if I was seriously injured. I didn't get to tarry long before a gruff voice bawled, "Are you going to lay there all day soldier?"

I looked up at a sergeant holding a clip board and writing my name. I said, "No sergeant" while hitting my quick-release button and struggling to my feet.

The sergeant ordered, "Then roll that parachute up and double time out of here."

Limping painfully, I tried to run. After I had gone approximately a hundred feet, the sergeant shouted, "Hey Martin, you passed!"

He must have been watching me all the time and realized that I had almost performed a miracle. The following morning at graduation ceremonies, I nearly popped my buttons with pride as my silver wings were pinned to my uniform. That afternoon, I boarded a train bound for Fort Campbell and a few hundred miles closer to Betty and Rodney.

Back at Fort Campbell, First Sergeant Bill Earhart was as good as his word. He installed me as Battery Clerk and I was immediately promoted to Private First Class. My responsibilities were to prepare all of the Battery's outbound correspondence, statistical reports, troop duty assignments, maintain the bulletin board, prepare the training schedule, and type the rosters of those scheduled to make jumps. I was truly enjoying my assignment and soon became respected as a member throughout the Battalion, wherein eventually I received promotion to staff sergeant.

Soon after returning from Jump School, I rented an apartment. The First Sergeant granted me a three day pass to bring Betty and Rodney to Clarksville. When she moved out of the Charleston house, her parents returned to their house at Smoot. Her college student sister, however, met and married her husband, so she remained in Charleston. With Betty and Rodney by my side, I felt whole once more.

Available housing in the vicinity was generally substandard, but by a true stroke of luck I rented half of a neat little duplex owned by the compassionate family of a building contractor. Their family, with whom we continue to stay in touch, made us part of their family. It was while living there, that our daughter Anita Sue was born June 23, 1952. I felt as though we were living in Paradise.

By living frugally, I was able to purchase a used car allowing me to commute to work. Although Korea was always on my mind, my assignment with Battery B was a genuine pleasure. My comrades also felt like family to me. The First Sergeant, who valued educational development, sent me successively to two Personnel Administration schools at Fort Benjamin Harrison at Indianapolis, Indiana. When I returned from the second one, Battalion Headquarters drafted me as the battalion Training Sergeant.

After all of the recalled Reserve troops had completed their refresher training and transferred to Korea, the 11th Airborne Division began intensive combat readiness training. Battery B along with all of the other Division Units made many mass jumps and drops of heavy equipment, including our jeeps and 105mm howitzers.

During the late fall of 1952, the entire 11th Airborne Division minus rear security personnel was airlifted to Camp Drum, New York for a three month long maneuver testing new cold weather clothing and equipment and to provide troop experience in near arctic conditions. A few days prior to the start of the maneuver, fifty two inches of lake effect snowfall threatened to delay the maneuver. Miraculously, a night-time thaw two days before the scheduled start reduced the snow to six inches of slush. The night before the start of the maneuver, the temperature dropped to twenty two degrees below zero. The slush then became six inches of glare ice. At 6:00 AM the next morning, I along with thousands of others exited our planes and was not sheltered beneath a roof until the end of March. Betty, Rodney, and Anita Sue, born June 23, 1952, spent the winter with her parents, while I imitated a polar bear along the St. Lawrence River.

During March of 1953, we made a mass jump onto seldom used drop zone Cooley, named for Sergeant John Cooley who lost his life there in a parachuting accident. The field was overgrown with scrub oak and briers. The weather was ideally dry, windless, and sunny. I was enjoying a great jump when, coming in backwards, I landed on the edge of a narrow dry creek bed and approximately ten feet of the bank's rim collapsed under my weight. I fell helplessly approximately six feet and folded tightly u-shaped into the contour of the banks with my head forced onto my chest on one side and my feet resting half way up the opposite bank. The impact forced my steel helmet forward scraping most of the skin from my nose. I was in terrible pain, but was able to exit the creek bed, pack my equipment, and walk to the assembly area. An X-ray revealed that I had cracked three vertebrae, one between my shoulders, another midsection, and one between my hips. I was told that I would only need therapy instead of surgery, so I continued my duties, although it required approximately eight years for most of the pain to subside. I learned how to cope with the problem, so fifty six years later, I seldom have a pain.

Near the end of 1953, the Army discontinued use of the World War II type T7 parachutes exchanging them for a more modern T-10 model. The T7 canopy was shallow and shaped like a saucer. When it opened the canopy came out the backpack first and the lines last. Attached to a fifteen foot long static line, the chute opened immediately behind the planes powerful engines. The opening shock was akin to being hit by a bus frequently causing painful abrasions upon the jumper's skin. The T-10 was described as a 'bag deployment' chute which is defined as the lines being displayed first and the canopy last allowing the jumper to fall far below the engine level. The opening shock was much less severe. Being shallow without a skirted edge, the T-7 was much easier to steer. The T-10 was shaped like a deep soup bowl and was difficult to steer, because the air would not easily spill from it during an attempt to guide it.

The approximate troop strength of an airborne division at that time was fifteen thousand men. The base Quartermaster Battalion was required to stock, pack, and maintain three times that many parachutes for both immediate issue and in reserve. Safety precautions required that every one of them had to be test jumped before general issuance to the troops. There was only one way that requirement could be accomplished; that was to have the best qualified jumpers to test them. I had by that time accrued enough jumps to be awarded my senior wings. Division Headquarters asked for volunteers comprised of those who had earned senior and master parachutist wings. There is nothing that gung-ho troopers would rather do than jump, so almost every qualified jumper in the 165th Airborne Field Artillery Battalion volunteered. Each of us was alerted by phone calls from the Battalion Training Officer to assemble at Headquarters when we were scheduled to participate. We boarded trucks and drew parachutes at the Air Base. We joked about the 'seven minute' flights. From the time the plane would leave the runway until the green light came on averaged about seven minutes. The airport was separated from Yamota Drop Zone by a chain-link fence. The planes reached twelve hundred feet of altitude, did a sharp right turn and we would jump. Most afternoons, each of us would jump twice. I personally jumped twenty two times one month.

As a consequence of the Korean War, men were individually transferred there and those who returned from combat duty replaced them in the Division. I expected to get the call at any time, but was never levied. The chances for promotion were nil, as those in combat deservingly received them. I, along with many other qualified men performed our duties in our current grades unselfishly. It was ironic that, when our Battalion Sergeant Major was promoted to Warrant Officer, all of the Battery First Sergeants, including our own, declined to fill the vacancy. They convened a meeting to determine a choice and unanimously nominated me, although I was only a staff sergeant instead of a master sergeant. Based upon my qualifications, I was made the acting Sergeant Major. Thus, being the superior Battalion non-commissioned officer by title only, I performed my administrative duties.

The constant threat of being sent to Korea not withstanding, Betty and I were content with our Army lives. The end of my three year enlistment was complete on December 12, 1953. A military career had not been in our plans, but the uneasy world situation with the Unites States committed to treaties with many countries intent upon curbing the threat of communism resulting 'brush fire wars' foretold that I may be dunked in and out of the Army indefinitely. We may never experience an uninterrupted civilian life. To better stabilize our immediate future, I re-enlisted for three more years.

During early 1954, the Division was given a mission to conduct basic training for thousands of two year draftees. Many of them wished to become paratroopers and we were given the option to retaining the most outstanding of them to replace our personnel losses to the war zone. Those became the best soldiers with whom I ever served.

One day, I was ordered to report for an interview with Brigadier General DeShazo, Commanding General of Division Artillery. He informed me that my reputation as a can-do would-do non-commissioned officer had attracted his attention. He said that he had a specific problem that he wished me to solve. He related that Battery B of a 155mm Airborne Artillery Battalion under his Command was in major trouble. That Unit was also conducting basic training, however, its Battery Commander, its First Sergeant, Supply Sergeant, and entire training staff had been engaging in fraud. Specifically, they were going to off post merchandise stores and, at the recruits' expense, were making profit by forcing them to completely duplicate all of their Government issued work uniforms. In addition, through collusion with the Supply Sergeant, they forced each recruit to purchase an individual rifle cleaning rod and were instructed that they must return them to the supply room upon graduation to be resold to the next inbound class. The morale of the recruits had sunk to bed-rock level. General DeShazo was receiving dozens of letters from irate parents and calls from The Inspector General in Washington to investigate the situation. Until replacements could be found, the Captain, his Executive Officer, Supply Officer, First Sergeant, and training NCOs were restricted to the Post pending Courts Martial.

The General was aware that I had reenlisted to fill the position I held as Sergeant Major, but he appealed for me for the good of the Division to accept transfer to the troubled Unit as First Sergeant. As a coincidence, a Master Sergeant returning from Korea was assigned to the 165th and I would have replaced me as Sergeant Major. The General told me that, due to the current promotion freeze, I would have to serve as an acting First Sergeant in my current grade for the time being. I was given the option of moving or staying with the Unit I had grown to love. I volunteered to accept his proposal and was transferred immediately.

I was injected into an awkward situation surrounded by the previous staff. As always required when a Unit Commander departed a command, the he was required to account for all of the Battery's Government supplies and equipment for which he had signed. On my second day of duty, he attempted to corrupt me by requesting that I go to the Quarter Master Supply Depot and requisition two hundred salvaged sheets under the pretense they would be used as cleaning rags. He said he could remove the areas stenciled 'SALVAGED' so he could return them to the Quartermaster as 'fair wear and tear', thus excusing himself from monetary liability. I flatly refused. He indignantly retorted, "I don't need your help. I've got a lot of pull on this Post." It was obvious to me that his 'pull' was what had gotten him into trouble in the first place. What was doubly shameful was that he violated the   ethics expected of  a West Point graduate.

The atmosphere was also tense with me having to be briefed by the indicted First Sergeant, who outranked me by one grade. It was necessary for him to reveal his duty rosters, personnel rosters, status reports, and trainee progress reports in order for me to perform my duties. His didn't hide his resentment for having to take orders from someone of lesser grade. He used every opportunity to show his immediate dislike for me, but that interlude soon passed as he and all of the others were confined to the stockade following their courts-martial.

Harmonious days arrived soon as Captain Madden fresh from combat in Korea took command. He soon earned my lasting respect as one of the most outstanding men I have known. In addition, combat experienced NCOs began to arrive and refilled our cadre. Once more, Battery B became Airborne proud.

During late spring of 1954, Betty's father was stricken with lung cancer. I took Betty and the children home to Smoot so she could help provide care and comfort to him and Betty's mother. He died a few weeks later at the age of seventy four years.

I was feeling stuck in a rut without probability of promotion, though fully qualified. I was grateful that I was never ordered to Korea where the war's progress also seemed to be stuck in a rut. Hoping to better myself with a career change, late in 1954, I applied for and was accepted at the Counter Intelligence Agent School at Fort Holibird, Maryland following an in-depth background investigation of my past. After graduation, I was transferred to the 11th Airborne Division Military Intelligence Detachment at Fort Campbell where I remained on jump status.

Beginning January 1955, the entire 11th Airborne Division was transferred to Germany with Headquarters at Augsburg. There were insufficient basing facilities to accommodate the entire Division so regimental and service Units occupyied Posts at Munich and Worms. All of the Division's heavy equipment was shipped to Germany by ship, but all personnel and family dependents were transported by plane from New York. The plane my family and I rode made a refueling stop at London in zero visibility fog. We were served lunch at the airport. The British are addicted to tea, but I ordered coffee, which I never received. When our waiter came to present our check, I informed him that I had not received coffee. With an indignant stuffy retort he stated, "You Yanks are very cranky about your coffee you know!" I never did get coffee.

We boarded a late afternoon train at Frankfurt and arrived at Augsburg near midnight. Approximately fifty inches of snow lay upon the ground. There was so much snow on the narrow streets the snow plows could only clear a single lane down the center. With nowhere else to put it, there were banks of snow six feet high on both sides of the streets. While riding a speeding taxi to our assigned apartment, meeting on-coming traffic was akin to traveling through a bobsled run with each vehicle literally sliding up the walls of snow to get by. The lateral tilt that resulted each time they met caused each of passengers us to pile atop each other. Our driver maintained his composure with complete aplomb throughout the trip.

Advanced planning by our Unit Commander prior to leaving Fort Campbell enabled our families to experience a turn-key entrance to our pre-assigned apartments. A member of the unit we replaced acted as my family's sponsor. He met us at the railroad station, guided us to our new home, and handed me the keys to our door. Back at Fort Campbell, we were directed to furnish a shopping list of basic food and other supplies we would need upon arrival. What a pleasure to enter warm rooms, find a stocked refrigerator, and beds prepared for sleeping.

After a few months, the Division was re-designated as the 23rd Infantry Division, but remained on airborne status. Except when engaging in tactical field operations or scheduled parachute jumps, my Intelligence Detachment colleagues and I were required to wear civilian clothing in order to conduct 'rank immaterial investigations' within the Military and also to be incognito during anti-communist operations among the indigenous population. Although being exposed to occasional moderate elements of danger, my duties were interesting and stimulating.

Our offices and bachelor quarters consisted of the entire top floor of a comfortable building named The Crossroads Service Club whose ground floor was home to a large Post Exchange restaurant. The building was located along a busy street and adjacent to and just outside one of our Army Bases. It was only one of four in the vicinity which did not show remaining bomb damage from WWII.

The Army provided our combination offices and bachelor quarters a 'House Frau' who used our kitchen to cook and serve the bachelor's meals and to perform janitorial service five days per week.

Our Detachment Commander was more than a little bit eccentric as also was one 'rookie' agent who was a Harvard graduate and whose home was in Massachusetts. He had a increasing rotund body and was generally not athletically disposed. I and most of his colleagues wondered how he graduated from 'jump school.' The first time any of our Detachment ever jumped from a C-130 plane was a night jump over Munich. I exited one door and he exited the opposite one simultaneously. I do not know if he struck a side of the plane or if the horrendous blast from the two engines on his side knocked him unconscious. He was out like a light when I observed him. With his weight being greater than mine, I was able to steer above him and follow him to the ground. I unhooked him from his harness and summoned a field ambulance. I visited him that evening at the Warner Barracks Dispensary where he regained consciousness near ten o'clock. He never knew what hit him.

I am mentioning all of the above this to lead into a story about that man's pedigreed Holenzolern German boxer dog, which he housed inside the bachelor quarters. That dog had to be the dumbest creature who ever lived, but his owner pampered him as though he was a baby. The dog had an insatiable appetite, so woe be unto anyone who left food unattended. The dog would eat it. Occasionally, someone would unintentionally leave the refrigerator door ajar. Once the dog's owner bought a half roll of bologna weighing approximately six pounds cased in a tight-fitting clear plastic wrapper. Desiring a late evening snack, he went to the refrigerator, but the bologna was gone. By morning the dog was in distress. As I arrived for work and saw a large group of Germans and soldiers observing an amusing show on the lawn of our office-building . There was the shivering dog humped over liken to a football center and the dog's owner wearing his black Army dress gloves in position like a quarterback attempting to pull the lodged plastic wrapper out of the dog!

We learned that our predecessors had discovered and accrued the names of a large number of communists among Germans residing in and near Augsburg, especially among union workers at a large truck factory and also an automobile factory. It was unproven if there were cells actively controlled by Russian interests, but we began monitoring their activities just in case the Soviets invaded and did activate the cells. American bachelor personnel frequented many of the German Gasthouses and dated German women. The manner in which our military bases were surrounded on all sides by the German communities, there was a constant possibility that some soldiers could become disaffected against the United States or become so compromised they may come under control of communist agents .

To better conduct liaison with the Germans, I was required attend a three month course at the Army's Language School at Oberammergau in beautiful southern Bavaria. I was, as were all the other students, assigned a private room to which I commuted approximately eighty miles following each week end. I joined a class of twenty two students, four of which were members of the Canadian Embassy at Bonn. I was the only class member who had not previously studied German or had grown in a family which spoke German. I hasten to state that competing with the others was difficult. Our instructors were native Germans who assigned us fifty new words to learn each day. I studied inside my room until two o'clock AM from Monday through Thursday and drove home at Augsburg each Friday evening. The class was graded on 'the Bell curve', which implied that there was a percentage of each class which would fail no matter how hard the student tried. I thought that was blatantly unfair. Out of a class of twenty two, I graduated eighteenth down from the top with a grade average of 91.9! I was amazed that I squeaked through.

By staying involved with my duties, I had accrued much unused vacation time and had allowed some of it to expire. To prevent further loss and to also tour beautiful and historical vacation spots with my family, we took one trip though western France, Luxemburg, the World Fair in Brussels, Belgium, and the tulip festival in Holland. One year later, we took a twenty one day camping trip through southern Bavaria, Austria, Italy, Liechtenstein, and Switzerland. Inside Italy, we toured Bologna, Venice, Florence, Rome, Naples, Pompeii, Pisa, and Genoa. I would like to have visited West Berlin, but due to our status, the Army forbade Agents from going there. We toured the canals of Venice and visited magnificent St. Mark's Cathedral. In Rome, we toured The Vatican, saw Pope Pius at St. Peter's Cathedral, stood upon the stage where Mark Anthony once made a historical speech, toured the Coliseum, the Pantheon, and the Catacombs. Traveling south to Naples thence to neighboring Pompeii, we climbed Mount Vesuvius inside our car and we entered its most recent volcanic crater. As we returned north along the beautiful Mediterranean Sea in balmy summer weather, we dressed only in our bathing suits in order to make frequent stops at excellent little roadside beaches. One day I picked up a small piece of driftwood that appeared to be mahogany. I took it home with me and have kept it on my desk to this day. With the Mediterranean being the basin receiving the rain, snow, and the runoff from the rivers of three continents, the origin of the driftwood intrigued me. I have, therefore, recorded my thoughts as follows:

## DRIFTWOOD

Long ago day-dreaming beside the
      Mediterranean Sea
On the shore of southern Italy
Consumed by thoughts of that historic place
So replete with events of the human race
At the water's edge where I stood
I spied a small piece of drifting wood
Later while holding it in my hand
I observed it was gnarled and etched by sea
      and sand

Musing, I wondered where it had grown
What native soil its roots had known
From whence it had arrived, by what random
    course
Dislodged by flood or quake of massive force
Helplessly born by wind and tide
Tempest tossed on endless ride
" Quo vadas?" a question in the tongue of
    ancient Rome
" Whither goest thou?" O vagabond searching
    for a home


Did it exit the Nile en route over Victoria Fall
Or the Dnieper through the Dardanelles
Come from the Barbary Coast, the South of
    France
Or float from the Blue Danube by chance
Did it come from a nation bordering this sea
Or was it by chance or providence it came to
    me
Had it spent only years or centuries upon the
    crest
Now a weary mariner seeking rest


As I pondered how the wood was by time
    abused
Wondered how, if ever, it had been used
A piece of oar once in the hand of a galley
    slave
Or a stick used by a Master to flog a knave

A shard of mast from a vessel storm-wrecked
      upon a spit
Or scrap from Cleopatra's barge or St. Peter's
      boat
Remnant from a hapless victim whom
      Barbary Pirates smote

Be it from ship, pier, mansion, hovel, or
      peasant's plow
Lush meadow, bog, glen, or lofty Alpine brow
Relic of the Greek Ionian Wars
The Crusades or Europe's conflicts with the
      Moors
Destined for so many years to roam
Upon Civilization's earliest commercial mains
Where many of three continent's rivers drain

What unseen spirits at that site with me stood
By me unheard their stories about that wood
Reality returned when a breeze rustled my
      hair
I glanced about to see if others were with me
      standing there
Alone in body if not in thought
I clutched my new found treasure that time
      forgot
Although to most it is a worthless chip
It reposes upon my desk lest I forget

We continued our journey north along the coast until arriving at the Leaning Tower of Pisa, the Italian Rivera, and to Genoa where we visited the Christopher Columbus birth place. We left Italy above Lake Como and passed through Switzerland, Liechtenstein, Austria, and reentered Germany at Lake Constance.

My assignment in Germany terminated during late December 1958 in time to be home for Christmas. My new duty station was at the Counter Intelligence Headquarters at Fort Holibird, Baltimore, Maryland. I was informed by the Personnel Officer that I would be assigned to a desk job there for the next five years. Being a field soldier, I hated the thought of that fate, so I contacted I one of my buddies working assignments at the Pentagon and asked him where I could be utilized anywhere else than Fort Holibird. He arranged a transfer for me to the Army Attache Department. Within days, I became a student at the Army Attache School at Fort Myers at Alexandria, Virginia. The course consisted of three stages: Attache Administration, Finance, and Photography. My projected assignment following graduation was to be US Army Advisory Group, Saigon, Viet Nam in February 1960. During the waiting period, I was placed on detached duty to a document library at CIA Headquarters at Langley where I transcribed classified documents to microfilm.

The Korean Presidential election was scheduled for April 1959. Sigmon Rhee, the sitting President did not wish to be replaced. During the campaign period, he had his opponents placed under house arrest. With the Demilitarized Zone between North and South Korea located approximately thirty miles north of Seoul and the cease fire pact tenuous at best, the US Government worried that the destabilizing effect of the President's action might create an opportunistic invasion by the Communists. The US Ambassador to Korea in union with the other Foreign Ambassadors, unsuccessfully urged the confrontational President to discontinue the house arrests and to conduct a free election.

My orders were immediately changed to a three year under-cover assignment to Army Attache, American Embassy, Seoul, Korea with a reporting date no later than Christmas Day 1959. My reenlistment date was December 12, 1959, so I could not leave for Korea until I reenlisted. The order provided that I could be accompanied by my family and that I could transport our family car. Being unable to depart prior to reenlisting, a firm port-call date of December 22 seemed improbable to keep during winter weather. Fortunately, we encountered no bad weather until arriving at Lake Tahoe. Listening to the news in a motel at Sacramento the next morning, I learned the road at Tahoe was closed to traffic after we passed. Our car was processed for shipment at the Port of San Francisco following which, we kept our port call date by boarding the plane which would carry us on a thirty three hour flight to Tokyo with stops at Honolulu and Midway Island.

We stayed overnight in Tokyo and caught a US Navy plane to Korea the next day. We were met at the Kimpo Air Force Base and taken to a hotel in Seoul. After the Christmas holiday, we were installed in the furnished house reserved for us at United Nations Village adjacent to Yong Dong Po six miles from the American Embassy in Seoul.

After getting settled in our home and having our children enrolled at the American School, I met my new colleagues at the Embassy. Once I was briefed and oriented about my mission and the responsibilities of a 'cover position' supervising the Attache limousine drivers, I surreptitiously began liaison with the CIA contingent in their quest to identify, defeat, and capture Communist infiltrators. Their sleeper cells, financed by counterfeit money, were dedicated to the disruption of the Korean Government during the controversy engendered by Sigmon Rhee.

The inflamed forces for and against him spilled into the streets throughout every city in South Korea. Riots and murders were rampant as the Army and National Police struggled to restore calm. Curfews were ignored as a shooting war raged day and night at Seoul. The American Embassy came under fire and the Ambassador's compound, United Nations Village, and the United Aid Mission housing areas and offices were placed under US Army protection and lock-down. We Embassy personnel were pinned down and confined to the Embassy for six days and nights without being able to communicate with our families because of no functioning telephone lines.

After a full week of riots, Sigmon Rhee conceded defeat and resigned as President by literally walking away from The Blue House Mansion in disgrace. Freed from house arrest, former university professor and Vice President Chong Myong became installed as temporary President until he won the position during the election.

Peace and quiet had returned to South Korea for a year under the gentle hand of the new president. One night, however, a power hungry Korean Army Colonel named Park Chung Hee, pulled his regiment from their position guarding an eastern segment of the Demilitarized Zone and striking at midnight committed a coup de grace installing himself as Dictator. Once more the Government was cast into turmoil. The American Ambassador, the 7th Army Commanding General, and The Director of United Aid Mission (USOM) refused to acknowledge the validity of the Dictator. Each resigned their positions, which caused USOM to withdraw from Korea and transfer to Indonesia.

With Pack Chung Hee racing up the middle of streets in his Army jeep equipped with a serine and flashing lights preceded by another with a mounted fifty caliber machine gun and followed by another acting like a pip-squeak Hitler, life in South Korea became a dull police state. Other vehicles, sometimes including those of our Embassy, had to climb curbs of narrow streets to avoid collision with that speeding idiot.

Betty and I remained in Korea an extra six months in order for our children to complete their school season, following which we returned home during July 1962. I was given the choice to fill any Attache vacancy for which I was qualified any place on earth, but I was tired of the house-bound feeling of no longer being Airborne. Therefore, I requested and was granted assignment to the 82$^{nd}$ Airborne Division Counter Intelligence Detachment at Fort Bragg.

# Chapter 10

# GOOD TO BE HOME

July's midnight temperature was still one hundred four degrees at Kimpo Air Base when my family and I boarded a plane en route to Japan. Upon arriving there, we were housed for two days at the Air Force Base guesthouse at Tachekawa awaiting a flight to Honolulu. My children had heard other American children tell about wild taxi rides in Japan. They were anxious for that experience them selves. It seemed that there were three classes of cabs. The most expensive were luxurious, slow, and not exciting. The middle class was fast and frisky. The cheep ones were slow, old, spiritless, and were no fun at all. Our kids urged us to hire one of the middle class to take us to the business center of Tokyo.

Now understand that the one we selected was not spiritless, but provided little seating space. Actually, the driver was the main ingredient of that experience. It became obvious that he had earned his driver license at a kamikaze demolition derby training school. The kids sat on the front seat while Betty and I shoe-horned ourselves into the tiny back seat space. When the driver fired that rocket with squalling tires, we could immediately sense that he was in a hurry. We begin traveling upon a two lane road with power line poles inserted into the curbs at the pavement edge. The fifty yard spaces between them were suitable for sidewalks, but that was where that maniac chose to drive astride the curb while cruising fifty miles per hour along side bumper to bumper traffic. What he did to avoid crashing into power line poles was amazing. He would drop off the curb and, crowd over towards the other cars. They would sway with no apparent rancor in unison like waltz partners without wrecking into him or each other. Having passed a pole, he would straddle the curb once more until reaching the next one. That Japanese roulette game lasted until we reached the shopping area of Tokyo, where major traffic circles began to appear filled by dizzying traffic. When I signaled the driver to stop before a toy store, he once more put two wheels upon the side walk casting pedestrians into shock. Shock also describes my condition as I paid the fare and attempted to walk upon weakened legs. My children were exhilarated and were off like a shot into the toy store, oblivious to the near-death experience we had just endured.

There was no way I was going to ride a taxi back to Tachekawa. Instead, we boarded a high speed 'bullet train.' The blur of the posted destination signs prior to reaching stations along the route printed in Japanese made me dizzy. Unable to either read or speak Japanese, I began to feel panic that I would not know when we reached Tachekawa. I expressed that fear to Betty and was overheard by an English speaking Japanese youth. What a relief when he kindly stated that he was familiar with the stations and would tell me when to pull the stop cable.

En route to Honolulu, our plane stopped at tiny Wake Island just as we had at Midway Island on our outbound flight. We reached Honolulu during a sunny mid-afternoon. There was a collective sigh from each of us as we passed by a pineapple cannery on our trip from the airport to Fort Durussey Army Guest House located at the middle Waikiki Beach. I am certain that I have never smelled a more delicious aroma. We vacationed there for two days before continuing our flight to Travis Air Force Base near San Francisco.

I bought a used car at Travis rather than using public transportation in order that we could tour interesting locations en route to our families at Smoot, West Virginia. Betty's oldest aunt on her Mother's side lived at Bakersfield, California. We had a reunion with her large family for two days before traveling on. Leaving California for home, we visited tourist attractions along the way including Sequoia National Forest, Hoover Dam, Grand Canyon National Park, Petrified Forest, and Crater National Park. We were having a great vacation through hot sunny July days. Outside the city limits of Little Rock, Arkansas, my children saw a sign advertising fantastic limeade at an upcoming restaurant. It being lunch time, we selected a table inside. A young teeny-bopper waitress came to take our order. She approached our table with a nonchalant 'I could care less' attitude while chomping upon what must have been a minute piece of chewing gum at one corner of her mouth. She looked appraisingly at us as though we were escapees from Mars. She spoke with the broadest nasal drawl I had ever heard as she demanded, "What y'all w-a-a-ant?"

I started to tell her that we wished to order lunch when she interrupted me with a snide smirk and asked, " Where y'all fro-o-o-om?"

I said, "We are from West Virginia."

With a snort, she slapped her thigh and said, "I thought it must be some funny place like that! Y'all talk so weird."

I decided that I was not any longer hungry, but I thought that I would give her something else to chew on. I said, "I'll have a duck egg and cabbage sandwich and a tall glass of buttermilk"

Obviously incapable of realizing that I was being insincere, she twanged, "We ain't got any of them the-e-ere."

I said, "I had my heart set upon having one, so we will just be moving on."

Nearby, we ate at a decent restaurant, which also served frosty glasses of limeade.

Having spent five years at Fort Campbell and Clarksville with our former landlord and friends, we visited them for two days learning what they had been doing. We made that our last stop before traveling the familiar pre-interstate two-lane roads through Kentucky to Ashland then US Route 60 through Huntington and Charleston to arrive at Smoot. We spent my thirty day leave with our families and neighbors, before reporting to my new assignment with the 82nd Airborne Division Counter-Intelligence (CIC) Detachment. We were displeased with the thin-walled on-post apartment we were assigned, so we bought and moved into a newly constructed brick house at College Lakes five miles from Fort Bragg.

I was pleased with my new assignment. The Detachment Commander, a major, was a role model of leadership. I was also pleased to learn that I would be serving once more with a former teammate at both Fort Campbell and Germany. We were reunited as a team.

Since I had not been on jump statue for three and one half years, I was required to attend a brief refresher period. When that was completed, nine flights of which were aborted because of storms at the scheduled jump sites, I began the think I would never make the necessary jumps to restore my airborne status. Soon after returning to Bragg, I applied for and graduated from Jumpmaster Leadership School during which I also earned my Master Parachutist wings. All of my duties with the 82nd Airborne CIC Detachment were in tactical support to the Division, both in garrison and on field maneuvers, therefore, we members dressed in field uniform every day with special insignia to distinguish our status.

Two major events occurred during 1963; the death of President Kennedy and the Bay of Pigs confrontation. We joined the remainder of the Nation with parades and other formal salutes honoring our fallen Commander In Chief. That was a sad time for all of us. As for the crisis in Cuba, the Division went on stand-by alert day and night for two weeks at a staging area until what threatened to become an invasion of Cuba evaporated. It was during that dust-up that I made my second jump of many from a C-130 Hercules Airplane. It was an awesome experience.

Demanding duties while serving in Korea caused me to forfeit eligibility for thirty days leave time three years in a row. I didn't want that to happen needlessly again so, during the early spring of 1963, my family and I began what we planned as a tour of Nova Scotia. We made an overnight rest stop in Baltimore. The weather report the following morning was that a major snow storm encompassed all of New England and Eastern Canada. Betty was unwilling to take the chance of it spoiling our vacation. We had never toured much of West Virginia, so we agreed to turn west and begin by visiting Brownsville, Pennsylvania, the town of my birth. My hopes were to discover some of my true relatives before concentrating upon West Virginia. I had learned from my birth certificate that I was born there and a letter written many years earlier by a former social worker, Mrs. Preston, had informed me that my mother had died there. I reasoned that there was a remote chance that perhaps I could locate the mortician who had buried her. I searched the telephone yellow pages and noted by advertisement the oldest established mortuary in Brownsville. We went there and interviewed the elderly owner of the mortuary and discovered that he not only buried her, he was a close friend and associate of both she and my father. He also said Father had owned a bus company with a route from Brownsville to Canonsburg. He said that soon after Mother's death, Father sold his business. He departed Brownsville with my two teen-aged brothers, Charles and Author, whom I do not remember ever seeing and have never located. Father never returned. The mortician said Mother was buried at the nearby Rosewood Cemetery. He also informed me that I had a female cousin living a few blocks away in town.

We went to the Rosewood Cemetery to search for Mother's grave, but due to its overgrown neglected condition with only a few permanent monuments, my search was futile. We visited my cousin afterward to learn as much as possible about my family, but she said that she was a child at the time of Mother's death and had no idea of where she was buried. She did say, however, that immediately following his discharge from World War II, Author appeared at her home unexpectedly and stated that he was en route to Baltimore to accept employment from Bethlehem Steel and would furnish her with his address as soon as he became settled. A letter never came.

Disappointed over being unable to locate Mother's grave, we returned to West Virginia traveling south via WV Route 19 and had decided that we would wait until almost dark before finding a motel. We passed through Morgantown, Fairmont, and were exiting the suburb of Monongah near 4:30 PM. The sun was low in the sky making visibility difficult for me when Betty said for me to turn about. She said we had just passed a business called Shinoskie's Meat Market, which I hadn't noticed. She wondered if that could be one of Uncle John's relatives. I parked in front of the store and noticed that it also doubled as the Monongah Post Office .

I entered the store where a woman near my own age was busy closing the Post Office for the day. Momentarily she asked, "May I help you?"

I told her that I was seeking information about the store's owner. I followed that by telling her that my name is James E. Martin and that I once had an uncle named John Shinoskie. Her face turned ashen as she grasped the edge of the counter top for support. I truly thought she was going to fall.

She shouted as she ran from behind the counter and embraced me, "Oh my God! You're Ebbie! We all thought you have been dead for all of those years! Don't leave. Wait until I close the Post Office. There is an old lady at that house on the hill across the road who will be thrilled to see you!"

I followed her car and, upon seeing the house among the Norway-spruce trees, I realized that it was Aunt Nell's house where I had attended those Saturday Night family gatherings as a little boy. Amelia, the postmistress near my own age, was Aunt Nell's only daughter. She sounded her car horn wildly upon approaching the house, causing the occupants to exit onto the lawn. There stood Aunt Nell with her snow white hair along- side handsome Uncle Stanley!

We hugged and cried and hugged some more, while Betty and the children gazed in awe. I hastened to introduce them and they too were engulfed with love. I told my relatives that I had so often recalled them and that house in dreams and reminiscence, wondering if I would ever see either again. After we were asked to enter the house, I requested Aunt Nell to take us through the basement entrance in order that I could see the room where those Saturday Night celebrations transpired so long ago.

There wasn't much sleep that night as the news of my reappearance spread by telephone among relatives over wide areas of the United States. Many were anxious to learn what happened after I was taken away form Uncle John, how I survived, and of where my long sojourn had taken me. Aunt Nell and Amelia were busy writing names and addresses of my parents' siblings as well as those of the Shinoskies. I was amazed to learn that my mother, Georgia Williams, her sister Blanche, and John Williams had emigrated with their parents from Wales and that my Martin grandparents had emigrated from Scotland with six sons and a daughter. Uncle John's two daughters and John Junior married and moved away. Avis, the evil witch, his second wife who had me separated from Uncle John's care, died within a few years after my departure. Uncle John moved to Detroit to live with his oldest daughter. He worked for Ford Motor Company where he lost his sight when a heavy hook swinging from an overhead crane struck him between his eyes.

I learned that my mother's brother, ninety year old John Williams, a retired railroad engineer, lived with his wife and two children at Majestic, Kentucky. That was only a partial list of the relatives about whom I had never known for over forty five years. I also learned that the sad eyed girl named Annie's family name was Fisher and that her married name became Swantek.

My family and I lingered in that enchanted place for a few days, before traveling to Davis, West Virginia to visit Annie. I was discouraged to learn that she was widowed and in poor health. We spoke of the old days and I promised to revisit her when I had the opportunity. Due to a later overseas assignment, I never had opportunity to make that return visit. During the interim, I learned that she had died.

Having detoured from our planned itinerary, we now passed from Davis through Elkins. Although it was hidden atop a hill behind many trees, I felt a shudder as we passed the orphanage where I had felt so imprisoned. I had no desire to stop. The only time I had traveled that road before it was unpaved. Now State Route 219 was paved all the way to Lewisburg and beyond. It was near midnight when we arrived at the home of Betty's parents at Smoot. We postponed any further tour of West Virginia, electing to stay with our old folk until time to return to Fort Bragg.

Life at Bragg was busy. Within a few days after we returned from leave, an Airborne maneuver named Operation Southern Pines involving most of the Division, began at Donaldson Air Force Base, Greenville, South Carolina. The maneuver area encompassed most of the agricultural and small town areas of Anderson, Greenville, Laurens, Newberry, and Saluda Counties, with the main drop zone at Joanna. We had a great time maneuvering against the 10th Mountain Division. The initial drop began at 6:00 AM on a bright Sunday morning. I exited over a two lane paved highway above a small frame house with a metal roof, a lean-to front porch, and a single short chimney made of brick.. I landed and rolled up my parachute when I observed a young trooper having jumped from the next 'wave' landing upon that house with a loud thump upon its metal roof. What happened next was spectacular. His feet rocketed across the down slope of the roof, then across the front porch roof, and his parachute snagged over that chimney, thus saving him form becoming injured. He came to a stop hanging midway between the porch roof and the porch floor facing the front door. The startled couple who lived there must have thought that a bomb had struck their house. They burst through the front door in amazement upon seeing that soldier hanging their. Possessing total aplomb, he smiled, waved, and said, "Good morning folks!"

Inside the village of Joanna, an irate woman heard a crash inside her vegetable-garden behind her house. She grabbed her broom and began beating what appeared to be some vegetable shrouded monster. When the debris was cleared from his body, she discovered it was her son.

Other than recruiting and debriefing informants to spy upon our 'enemies', there was not much for my colleagues and I to do. As we lived among our hosts, they enjoyed all of the excitement the maneuver had brought to their communities, so, serving as our informants, relished playing Sam Spade and Joe Friday for the duration of the maneuver.

One warm mid-afternoon, a fire fight broke out between the opposing forces at a small bridge that spanned the Saluda River. The Umpires had completed their assessment of who had won and lost. Our paratroopers lost. The umpires erected a sign on both approaches of the bridge, 'Warning: This Bridge Is Destroyed. Do Not Use.' Also, the medics tagged various soldiers as walking wounded, seriously wounded, and dead. They were told to remain there until ambulances would arrive to take them to a field hospital. The soldiers did what all good soldiers do. They lay upon the ground and slept. An elderly lady, who obviously did not understand the make believe war happening within her neighborhood, parked her car and aroused a soldier upon whose shirt a bright red tag was attached. She asked, "Does that sign on the bridge mean what it says, Sonny?"

Without moving, the soldier responded, "You shouldn't be talking to me Lady. I'm dead."

All good things eventually come to an end, so the evening before the maneuver ended, our Detachment Commander radioed that he wanted all Agents to assemble at his field headquarters the next morning in preparation to return to Bragg. In his message, he cordially invited us to eat breakfast with him. His tents were pitched inside a small untilled field overgrown with tall weeds, scrub-oak, and dwarfed jack pines. The location was less than one hundred fifty yards from a cluster of sub-standard farm-shacks, hog pens, and farmyard chicken lots.

As usual, the major was in a jovial mood. His headquarters had remained at that location throughout the entire maneuver, so he had made friends with the local residents. Obviously, they were pleased to have so much excitement happening near their normally sleepy village. Someone had provided a thin steel rod with a hook at one end. The opposite end was driven into the ground, enabling the soldiers to heat water over a fire by using a steel pot dangling from the hook. They used the water for making coffee and for shaving, but the most remarkable use of it was for boiling eggs.

The major was sitting upon a folding steel chair as he said, "Help your selves to breakfast. The boiled eggs are fresh and are excellent."

Excellent indeed! The first two I cracked contained un-hatched chicks. The major admonished, "Don't worry, there are plenty more." That offer didn't sound appetizing to me, so I returned to eating my field rations.

With the maneuver over, the Division returned to Fort Bragg. Throughout the years that I served with my teammate, he had owned an electric coffee pot. He believed that a coffee pot should never be scrubbed. He said  doing so altered the taste of the brew.  He faithfully prepared coffee every morning for the entire detachment. The resulting product never poisoned any one, so we humored him. One morning a newly assigned second lieutenant took one look at that pot and cleaned it to a gleaming shine with steel wool. All of we others awaited with gleeful anticipation my partner's arrival. When he started to make coffee, he erupted. He backed the offender into a corner and warned him to never touch his coffee pot again. I mention this because we chided him almost daily about his grungy pot. He learned that I was going on a four week temporary duty assignment to attend Lie Detector School at Fort Gordon, Georgia. The day I departed, he emptied the left over coffee into my personal cup, following which he stored my cup inside my top desk drawer to await my return. Once more there was a gleeful audience upon my return watching to see my reaction. I was amazed to discover a weird multicolored mutation, which had reached an inch above the brim of the cup. In jest, my buddy clapped me on the shoulder and said, "Drink up. I always look out for you."

The temporary duty assignment referenced above was ordered by the Major. He wanted every Agent to become proficient in as many aspects of our profession as possible, so he scheduled me to attend The Lie Detector School. When I returned to Bragg after graduation, I was amazed to learn that our Detachment was ordered to transfer to the 1st Airborne Brigade, Eighth Army Headquartered at Bad Kreuznach, Germany. I suspected that the Major and First Sergeant had conspired to cause that transfer, because both loved previous assignments to Germany. Furthermore, five of the other Agents, including myself had also served there. The intrigue of counter- acting mischief of the Russians and many German Communists was much more interesting than mundane document security and personnel background investigations at Bragg. My suspicion was also strengthened, when out of the blue, both my partner and I received orders to attend the six week Defense Again Sound Entry (DASE) course at Fort Holibird, Maryland en- route to Germany. The course was a detailed study of the most modern electronic listening devices. Our wives and children were to join us with the remainder of Detachment upon our graduating. To prevent my partner and I from losing jump pay in transit, we made an overlapping jump before leaving Bragg.

To disclose the can-do-self reliance of Army wives, Betty arranged the storage of our furniture, rented our house to a tenant, closed our utilities, cleared the Post, up-dated our passports, had our family dog's inoculations renewed, made the necessary arrangements for our car to be shipped overseas, and attended my graduation.

When the 11th Airborne Division CIC Detachment transferred to Augsburg, Germany during February 1956 we were billeted in the Saint George Hotel, New York City following which we traveled via plane from LaGuardia. This time, after shipping our car, we caught passage on the Navy's troopship USS Darby at the Brooklyn Navy-yard. The Darby was a magnificent ship upon which my family and I had returned to America from our previous assignment in Germany. Having my feet back aboard the Darby again was like visiting an old friend. My only disappointment was that my long-time team mate received a change in assignment orders and did not accompany us to Germany. I have never seen him again.

# Chapter 11

# GERMANY REVISITED

The members of our Detachment, our families, and pets settled comfortably into a cruise aboard the Darby. Its first port of call was at Groton, Connecticut to load a contingent of Navy Seabees being reassigned to a base at a small harbor in Spain, which the Navy referred to as Rota. The weather was beautiful every day and night of the voyage. Passengers busied themselves walking the decks of the seven hundred eighty foot ship, using exercise equipment, playing cards, feeding and walking their pets, watching sea life playing, and enjoying the night-time entertainment. Life was good.

On day six, we arrived at Rota. Two days were spent transferring the newly arrived Seabees and their equipment ashore following which the home-bound Seabees and their gear came onboard the Darby. We Army personnel and our families were not permitted to leave ship. The morning of the third day, the Darby was backed from the pier into the harbor, however, by some miscalculation, the tugboat crews allowed the stern of the ship to run aground upon a sandbar. Several hours passed before the ship was freed. More hours were spent as divers inspected the propellers and steerage to determine if damage had occurred. It was after dark before the ship exited the harbor. The ship sailed north skirting the French coast until entering the English Channel. At sunrise we were treated to a grand view of the White Cliffs of Dover. Late that evening we arrived at Bremmerhaven, Germany our port of debarkation.

We boarded a train, which transported us to the U.S. 8th Army Headquarters at Bad Kreuznach, where our designated Unit was located. Agents were assigned responsibilities to the far-flung Units of the 1st Airborne Brigade as well as the 8th Army. My family and I were provided vehicular transportation to a Army tank range at the small Nahe River Valley village named Baumholder. Baumholder is not a scenic place, but the nearby village of Ideroberstein located four miles away in the wine-producing Nahe Valley has a most spectacular granite peak arising from the valley floor immediately adjacent to a paved highway. Carved into the peak's sheer face is the façade and interior of a tall cathedral accessible only by many steps also chiseled into the stone, a project which must have required many decades of arduous labor to complete.

My family and I were provided an apartment within a Government housing area and our two children attended an American staffed school.

Two existing agents were assigned the Baumholder office, one which was also a paratrooper. I was immediately pressed into my new duty assignments. Much of my time became consumed being transported by helicopter to two other firing ranges many miles north of Nurnburg near the Czechoslovakian border. Many of the Units stationed at Baumholder spent month long maneuvers throughout the year at those much larger firing ranges in near proximity to the 'Iron Curtain'. Communist infiltration was a constant threat to be defended against. In spite of Baumholder's remoteness and small size, I became involved in two significant investigations involving Communist attempts to involve our soldiers in espionage and disaffection during my assignment there.

After thirteen months of duty at Baumholder, I was assigned as Station Chief of the Maintz Field Office located across the Rhine River from Wiesbadden. That was one of the choicest assignments in all of Germany. Our office was situated in a corner of an Army compound with a private fenced enclosure including a secure parking lot for our jeeps and field equipment. Two young bachelor Agents assigned to that station had living quarters with complete facilities on the second floor above our office. Neither were airborne qualified, but were efficient, thus making my job pleasant.

Two blocks distance, my residential quarters were in a modern duplex upon a beautiful street, surrounded by shade trees, a manicured lawn, large windows, and a view of the Rhine River. The American elementary school attended by our daughter, was located two blocks from our residence. Our son, who was a high school senior, traveled daily by school bus across the Rhine River to Weisbadden, the location of the U.S State Department's boarding school for children of its diplomats at Bohn. Children of Army personnel and those of a large contingent of Air Force personnel assigned to the busy Wiesbadden airfield also attended that school. Our son graduated in a class of more than six hundred students the same year of my assignment at Maintz.

There were no airfields in the vicinity of Bad Kreuznak, so some of us members of the 1st Airborne Brigade stationed at the Division's various satellite locations renewed our three month proficiency requirements by jumping from 'Huey' helicopters atop a hill named Kuhberg (Cow Hill) just outside the city limits. Seven would sit upon the floor and, when told to exit, one at a time would scoot into the open doorway, place feet upon the landing skids, and bunny hop into the air. What a great life!

There were two personally memorable mass brigade size jumps in which I participated. One was near a small German town named Dexheim, a grape and sugar beet producing area. The first occurred near a large vineyard where a sudden gust of wind carried many jumpers off course. The posts supporting thousands of grape vines stood in long rows approximately ten feet apart. Our interesting task was to avoid being impaled upon the posts upon landing.

The other memorable jump for me occurred near Stuttgart during the sugar beet harvesting season. Many growers were busy transporting their harvest to a central point where a pulverizing mill would be temporarily positioned. That huge field also was the one selected as our drop zone on that date. Dozens of farm wagons loaded with the large beets were being unloaded forming ricks approximately twenty feet long by ten feet wide and eight feet in height.

Weather conditions throughout Germany are notorious for sudden changes. Although the sun was brilliant that afternoon, a strong wind developed almost the moment the mass drop began, thus blowing our parachutes off the intended course. A friend and I were the last jumpers to exit our plane from opposite doors. We were blown near the end of the drop zone and almost directly above the working farmers, who must have become so accustomed to parachute jumps, they ignored our shouts of warning. My friend landed atop one of the huge ricks located amid a cluster of wagons. The impact caused the pile of beets to collapse, causing him to pitch off landing head first. The impact with the ground drove one of his shoulders partially into his rib-cage. I came dangerously close to kicking several men and women on their heads as I raised my feet to avoid them. I missed the beets, tractors, and wagons, but my landing was completely out of control as I was dragged along the ground by my fully inflated parachute. I managed to rise to my feet, having performed a recovery from the drag maneuver, but I was traveling too fast to avoid falling. I was carried beyond the cleared field into one which had not been harvested. The domes of the beets extended at least a foot above the soil and the juicy leaves of the plants were up to my arm pits. Remaining afoot was impossible as my shoes slid off the juicy domes. Each attempt of recovering from the drag resulted in falls in which my reserve parachute flew upward exposing my rib-cage to painful bruises. I finally quit attempting to stand after one of the beets broke two of my ribs. I was being pulled along so fast I feared that the beets would also break my neck, so I locked each of my elbows beneath my tightly packed reserve parachute attached to my harness below my chin and I remained in that position until reaching the edge of a small hill. Once I passed the crest, the parachute deflated from lack of wind. I hastily stowed my parachute inside its kit bag and, painfully, I rushed back to check the condition of my friend. The paramedics had arrived and were loading him into a field ambulance. He survived, but he experienced a long recovery period. As pertained to myself, I fully recovered after a few weeks.

One of my interesting assignments while stationed at Maintz involved a two week daily commute to 8th Army Headquarters where I was placed in charge of three other men appointed by the Division G2 to develop the Intelligence Annex Plan for a June NATO maneuver at Boris, located on the North Sea costal plain of Denmark. We were informed at an initial briefing that the 1st Airborne Brigade was to become a surrounded hostile invasion force pitted against the Danish Home Guard in collusion with the Queen of England's favorite troops, the British 1st Scott Fusiliers. The purpose of the brief maneuver was to better train the Danes in defense of their country during the Cold War threat. The scenario was that we paratroopers were to be repulsed and defeated within three days after landing. Being defeated at any time just is not an acceptable condition in any paratrooper's mind. Never the less, we followed orders and developed a plan. I was apprehensive about our lack of infrastructure information surrounding the maneuver area, having gleaned little from available map studies. It would be useful to have knowledge provided by an infiltrator, if one could be had. Knowing that American school teachers stationed in Germany would be beginning vacations in June, many of whom would use the time touring Europe, I located two young men who were interested in visiting Denmark, and especially to have an opportunity to observe a mass parachute jump. They gleefully agreed to act as our eyes and ears. I gave them instructions to avoid encounters with Danish officers, who may have them arrested on suspicion, but rather to concentrate upon young boastful enlisted men anxious to demonstrate how important they were. Our infiltrators were amazed by the willingness of the Danish soldiers to discuss the pending maneuver, allowing our surrogates to visit their pubs and military facilities. We instructed them to meet us for a debriefing upon the Brigade's arrival at the Danish Tirstrup airfield. There were periods of rain which caused some delays, but June 18, 1965 became sunny permitting the first paratroopers to land and secure the drop-zone before nightfall. A total of three thousand men made the jump, with the flight in which my unit jumped landing at midnight. Boris is located far enough north that day light lasts almost twenty four hours at that time of year. The upper rim of the sun is slightly visible on a clear night as it passes across the horizon from west to east. I could have read a printed page without a light at midnight when I arrived upon the ground. My jump was uneventful except that I felt a hard object beneath my right hip upon landing. Since there was no wind, my parachute collapsed over me. I found the object and examined it, discovering that it was a smooth stone measuring approximately five inches long and resembling a small hammer without a handle. It had groves ground into the circumference of its midsection as though to accommodate a cord. Furthermore, one peen surface contained a large chip as though it had struck something with great force. I immediately conceived that my souvenir must have been a battle hammer lost during an ancient mid-evil battle. Later, I attached a handle to it and it rests atop my office desk to this day.

The maneuver proceeded as planned and our Brigade was defeated as planned. It would have been a pleasant experience had a heavy cold rain not begun shortly after midnight following our landing. Our only food supply was the few combat rations each trooper carried inside his back-pack. The plans were that we would be resupplied by air-drop each morning, but zero visibility persisted the entire maneuver period preventing the planes from flying. I allowed myself approximately two ounces of beans and meat from my field rations at six o'clock both morning and evening until the sunny morning when the maneuver ended.

Our sector of the maneuver area was overgrown by waste-high heather which was almost impossible to walk through. We were drenched to our skin and had nothing with which to create a fire. Our ponchos protected our upper bodies, but the forty degree wind-driven rain and every step through the sodden heather brought rivers into my boots night and day. To attempt sleeping upon the ground inside a pup-tent and a soaked sleeping bag was impossible as was sleeping at all.

But… the maneuver ended as planned and we survived. What a relief to return to my cozy office at Maintz.

A former colleague and his family from the Army Attache Office at Seoul, Korea became assigned to the American Embassy at Bohn, a short day-trip from Mainz. My family and I enjoyed a few week-end vacations visiting those friends. Our route along the Rhine River passed the ruins of the famous World War II Remagen Bridge and the fabled Lorelei Cliff.

It was at Maintz that Betty, my wife, began experiencing a serious medical problem. It was also at that time I received orders to transfer to Headquarters and Headquarters Company, 66th Intelligence Battalion at Stuttgart, Germany. I was given a promotion to First Sergeant E-8 and replaced the current First Sergeant who was entering retirement. That assignment took me permanently off parachute status, much to my regret after making two hundred forty successful jumps.

I began enjoying my new assignment, but it was not without some difficulties. Visiting hundreds of rooms throughout that old fort along with my many other duties took some time. Typical of German architecture, the third floor of those buildings were topped by huge attics with steep tile covered roofs. The attics contained large double-sash windows installed inside dormers and were located approximately twelve feet apart. Over time, many window panes had become broken without replacements. There was little reason for anyone to visit those attics, so they had been neglected.

Two events within a month of my arrival truly caught my alarmed attention to the attics. Our Battalion was into both intelligence gathering and counter-intelligence business with heavy concentration upon international affairs pertaining to the Soviet Union and the 'Iron Curtain.' Our Company had members who were 'penetration agents' working behind the Iron Curtain. Although I never expected to meet any of them, they were assigned to our unit and I was responsible for their administrative needs. The only time I met any of them was when some arrived to be debriefed by their handlers. A small second floor room located above the offices of Battalion Headquarters was provided as their sleeping quarters during the visit. One man came to see me the morning following his arrival to request another room, because   a terrible stench from behind an attic door. He had opened that door for what must have been the first time in decades.

He requested that I accompany him for a view of what he had seen. I agreed, and when I opened that door, I saw at a depth of half the door's height and corresponding to the slope of the stairs and disappearing beyond my view was a solid bed of pigeon guano and nests of both living and dead squabs. I was in shock! My imagination of the attics of all of those huge buildings being likewise filled coupled with the obvious task awaiting me blew my mind. I immediately moved the men to a clean second-floor room and requested that both the Battalion Commander and my Company Commander to witness the situation. They summoned members of the local Base Engineers to observe it. The Engineers agreed to provide dump trucks, tools, laborers, masks, and other necessary sanitation equipment to begin removing the guano the  next day. They had to create corridors made of sheets of plywood and covered by tarps across troop rooms and along stairways in order to suppress the spread of dust as the guano was being removed. They worked methodically to protect the base mess-hall, troop quarters, and offices from both dust and germs. Weeks were required to clean the attics and to replace broken window panes.

Our small fort contained an enlisted men's club to which famous music and movie stars assigned to the USO troop entertainment program visited upon an almost weekly basis. Among those whom I saw were Roy Acuff, Buck Owens, Jimmie Dickens, and others. The Drifters arrived to perform the night of July 3, 1965. Our Battalion planned an all day Fourth of July celebration with a picnic and an inter-mural softball game. We invited the Drifters to remain and celebrated with us. The softball game was a blast!

Soon after the guano removal began, a personnel sergeant assigned to duty at the Battalion Headquarters disappeared. Although his co-workers had not observed that had been acting strangely, he was known to be an excessive drinker of intoxicants. In addition to an all points missing person report having been issued, a person investigating the progress of the guano removal discovered the sergeant hanging by a rope tied to an attic rafter above a stairwell.

Although I had never completed a death report, fate was to change that for me in rapid succession. Soon after the sergeant committed suicide, the date of the annual visit by an Inspector General was announced. All sections of the Battalion were busy hoping to earn a passing grade. We tried to relieve some of the strain of all that had happened by scheduling some recreation into our duties to keep morale as high as possible. One Saturday, an Infantry Company invited our Unit to play them a game of baseball upon their field located two miles distance from our fort. All had a good time with soldiers and their dependents acting as fans. One of our young men had ridden his motorcycle to the game. While returning to our base via a one-lane tree lined road, he lost control and crashed into a tree. He was dead at the scene. Late that same afternoon, one of our young corporals returning from vacation lost control of his car exiting the Autobahn and broke his neck. One night later, a sergeant who worked at Battalion Headquarters had spent the evening after supper painting his second floor room in preparation for the Inspector General's arrival. Somehow a fire ignited inside his room. Later, he stated that some of his siblings died when the family home burned during his early life. In the process of painting his small room, he had blocked the door to the corridor with furniture. In panic, he jumped from a window. He landed on his feet striking a concrete revetment that surrounded a basement window, driving one of his thighs into his chest cavity. He also survived in a gravely serious condition following evacuation to a trauma center located at Fort Gordon, Georgia.

Concurrent with those disasters, every Section of our Command teemed with Inspector General staff-members and investigative personnel auditing our compliance with Army regulations. Fortunately for us, we received a favorable report.

Fate was not finished with us, for my wife's condition required emergency surgery. Upon completion of her operation, she was immediately evacuated to Walter Reed Army Hospital, Washington, DC. She was transported in the same hospital plane as our two injured soldiers. Orders were written for me and my children to follow her. I was fortunate that my children were mature enough along with the help of colleagues and kind neighbors to survive and do their part to make the move. I, on the other hand, could have benefitted by being triplets. I had to pass the clearing of quarters inspection, arrange the shipping of our belongings, had to recruit a qualified sergeant to replace me, hurriedly brief him about the conduct of his new responsibilities, inventory the Company's classified documents, and drive my car to Bremmerhaven port to be shipped to the Brooklyn Navy Yard. Following that, I returned to Stuttgart by train.

That time was mid December and I was experiencing the most devastating bout of influenza of my life. The officers and enlisted men with whom I had worked gave me a rousing go-away party, but I was so racked by fever, pain, and congestion that I was barely aware of it. I, my children and our dog, Weinersnitzel, were driven to the Frankfurt Airport by one of our good friends with whom we stay in contact to this day.

I was a zombie aboard the plane to Fort Dix, New Jersey. After arrival, we rode a bus to Washington where we joined my wife at Walter Reed Army Hospital. She had an aunt and uncle who lived in nearby Silver Spring, Maryland. They invited the children and I to reside at their house for the Christmas Season and as long thereafter as necessary. I had been granted a thirty day leave so that I could make arrangements for my family before going to my new duty assignment at Pittsburg. Two weeks after arriving at Walter Reed, Betty was discharged.

Without knowing how long Betty would have to stay in the hospital, we made the decision to send our two children to Greenville, South Carolina to live with Betty's sister and her family until we could settle into my new assignment. I accompanied them to the Washington bus station where they boarded a Greyhound bus. I was apprehensive about entrusting two teenagers traveling alone for such a long distance, but their success completing that trip reveals how self reliant Army Brats can be. They made the trip without a glitch, including an exchange of bus at Charlotte, North Carolina.

Following her release from Walter Reed, Betty and I boarded a train en route to White Sulphur Spring, West Virginia, arriving during a blizzard. My foster father, Cecil, met us at White Sulphur Springs, West Virginia and took us over treacherous snow drifted country roads to our home farm on Little Sewell Mountain. Betty and I travelled to Greenville, South Carolina to rejoin our children at Betty's sister's home. Within a few days, I returned to the Brooklyn Navy Yard to retrieve our car. I returned my family to Smoot to stay with Betty's parents, while I traveled by bus to Pittsburg to join my new assignment with the 109th Military Counter-Intelligence Detachment on the top floor of the Liberty Building. After duty hours, I began searching for living quarters for my family.

I was given no free time to locate a place to live as I began receiving assignments and was placed into service immediately. A new colleague was scheduled for retirement in two weeks. He was the only person who showed compassion for me being afoot in a totally unfamiliar city and with only after-duty hours to search for a place to house my family. He had an unused bedroom in his apartment which had already been leased to a new occupant. He reasoned that I should be able to locate a place to live before he was scheduled to depart.

Both of us rode the Castle Shannon trolley to and from work each day. The Federal Bureau of Investigation occupied the next level of the Federal Building below our offices and we shared the elevators at quitting time each evening. I observed that a few of the FBI men also rode the Shannon trolley. One evening I asked them if they knew of any available housing where they lived. Luck was with me. One of the men said that he lived within two hundred feet of the trolley stop at Mount

Lebanon, he had a wonderful apartment, and he was vacating it within a week to accept a new assignment. He gave me the name and telephone number of the rental agent controlling the leasing of that building. I called and obtained the lease the following day.

So my tracks on foreign soil ended along with the retirement of my paratroop jump-boots. I would have enjoyed finishing my Germany tour if unforeseen circumstances not intervened and I would have also enjoyed prolonging my parachuting career on future assignments. I am extremely happy that Betty recovered completely. Now my family, possessions, and our dog would soon be reunited in the setting of an exciting new adventure upon US soil.

# Chapter 12

# PITTSBURGH

After the FBI Agent evacuated the apartment, I had the utilities assigned to me. It would be two or more weeks before our furnishings would arrive. In the meantime, I called my father's brother, Bill Martin to inform him that I had arrived in Pittsburgh. Although we had previously corresponded from locations where I had been assigned, we had not met. He provided directions to his residence and invited me to visit. He and his wife, Lois; his daughter Jean; his son Bill, Jr. and Bill's wife Gertrude welcomed me. I spent several evenings with them. The remaining time I could utilize my Army friend's apartment was waning. Jean, a spinster, had an apartment with unused rooms at nearby McKee's Rocks. She invited and I accepted her invitation to live there until my furniture arrived at our apartment on Liberty Avenue at Mt. Lebanon. Our household shipment soon arrived as expected and our family was reunited inside our new residence. Betty was recovering from her surgery, our daughter, Sue, enrolled at the Mount Lebanon Elementary School located within a short walking distance from our home, and son, Rodney, obtained a job with a local Buick dealership. He worked there until being drafted into the Navy.

Visual orientation was confusing for me upon getting my first overviews of the junction of the Allegheny and Monongahela rivers forming the Ohio River at the Point District as seen from the top floors of the Federal Building.. I was provided an Army sedan for transportation and detailed maps from which I recorded the street addresses of my assignments prior to leaving our offices. Although my territory was vast, with assistance from my teammate, I soon learned my way about the area.

Our Pittsburg Office was truly busy throughout the two and one half years of my assignment. I inherited a full case load in-box with completion dead-lines. Aside from my daily liaison duties at the Headquarters of the Pittsburg Police Department, most of my work pertained to background investigations of Army and civilian personnel being considered for government security clearances allowing access to sensitive classified documents and materials.

One of my most lengthy assignments involved taking sworn statements from highly placed steel executives when the suitability for a top secret clearance of one of their own was strongly contested by several of his colleagues and  acquaintances. Since the Subject was rather young by comparison to other corporate executives among the several steel corporations for whom he had worked, had demonstrated ruthlessness in his climb up corporate ladders, and had earned the reputation of being a 'hatchet man', He hadn't made many friends. That investigation resulted in my visiting the corporate offices of every steel corporation in the region. That case became tedious for me, because each negative interview had such legal implications that sworn statements had to be recorded in print. Preparation of the typewritten sworn statements on legal sized paper had to be done without any blank spaces, but rather, typed to all  side edges , tops, and bottom edges of each page and each one initialed by both myself and the interviewee including his signature. There could be no room for contesting the agent report.

Since I had to fit my appointments into the available time(s) of the interviewees, much of my time had to be sacrificed from other assignments pending in my caseload. The Department of the Army Intelligence Headquarters at Fort Meade, Maryland constantly expressed impatience for me to complete my report about the steel executive. That day finally came, but I was amazed several weeks later to see the Subject's full-page picture on the front cover of a national magazine announcing that he had been promoted to President of the steel corporation for which he worked.

I kept extremely busy while stationed in Pittsburg. My in-box atop my desk was constantly full. My investigations took me inside many homes, schools, garages, factories, offices of professional athletic teams, and one chicken packing house. Although I was regarded with occasional suspicion by interviewees in the ghetto sections of various communities where people are reluctant to reveal information about acquaintances, I seldom encountered difficulty.

Most of our Unit's normal duties became suspended because of the civil disturbance caused by the Martin Luther King assassination. As happened throughout the Nation, Pittsburgh came under lethal attack by raging gangs. The first riots in Pittsburgh came as citizens of the northern part of the city, known as the 'Hill District', began destroying City property and burning most business within their community. They also began a massive march with intent to destroy the Pittsburgh's Business Center by fire, looting, and general rampage. A state of emergency was immediately declared, the National Guard was activated, and in unison with the city police force, they thwarted invasion of the city center by holding a line south of the 'Hill District.' Pittsburgh's Mayor declared a curfew and established a 'War Room' at Police Headquarters. I and my team-mate were assigned to the 'War Room' on twelve hour shifts per day every day and night for the duration of the riots. We sat at long tables equipped with numerous telephones and radios being manned by FBI Agents, Police Departments, Members of City Council, firemen, and news reporters. The Pittsburg line continued to hold, while the rioters reportedly began to suffer hunger, having destroyed their sources of food by fire. Months following the riots, shoppers aboard city busses coming from and returning to the burned out Hill District could be seen with full shopping bags held upon their laps. In Army parlance, burning of the Hill District was tantamount to calling artillery fire upon their own foxhole. Lesson learned: Building contractors and other businessmen were reluctant to reestablish there.

While the mule trains from the South were desecrating the parks and the reflection pool area between the Nation's Capitol and the Lincoln Memorial in Washington, our Huntington Team was being acclaimed as heroes for detecting that a truck loaded with TNT intended to be used to destroy the city center of Pittsburg was intercepted and impounded along with its crew. West Virginia Governor Hulett Smith was elated and so were we in Pittsburg. Fortunately for all, the riots abated soon afterward and life returned to normal.

My family enjoyed our quaint old-fashioned duplex apartment. We made friends with our neighbors and spent free times and picnics with my relatives. After hours from their day- jobs and on a couple of week-ends, Bill Jr., Gertrude, and Jean assisted Betty and I repainting our new home. The residential property of the owner of a Mt. Lebanon butcher shop joined on the backside. He was an avid horse shoe pitcher who had built a professional quality horse shoe course on his back lawn. He usually had to pitch alone until I became his neighbor. I spent many happy evenings after work with him.

During the time before our son went to the Navy, he developed friends among other musicians. As he did in Germany, he formed a five piece band and spent week-ends traveling to play at Seven Flags and other venues. It was while following that endeavor that he met his future wife, Sharon Purvis. When Rodney entered the Navy, the emptiness of his absence caused us to feel as so many other American parents must have upon seeing their sons leave home to uncertain future.

I am certain that it was coincidental, but it seemed that I always arrived at a new Unit assignment just in time for the annual Inspector General's visit. Being at Pittsburgh was no exception. There was very little of a material nature within our offices of desks, chairs, book cases, cabinets, typewriters, and files. The exceptions were our assignment of Army sedans. There is not much can be done to make dull non-luster Army olive drab green paint look good, but the interior and mechanical conditions plus maintenance records are a more important matter. Being the senior 'go-to' for overseeing the task, I immediately taught all of the 'young bucks' of the Organization vehicle maintenance 101. We were allocated one week to render the sedans ship-shape. In testimonial to our success, we received official recognition when the IG report stipulated that was the first time during the past six years that the motor pool passed inspection!

As had become traditional with me being submerged into my duties, I seldom used my entitled yearly leave time, thus losing most of it. Such was my stay at Pittsburgh. I enjoyed spending time with my family, my Pittsburgh relatives, and learning much family history from Uncle Bill. He had been a member of the US Navy during World War I. He once commented to me that he was in the Navy when it was manned by iron men aboard wooden ships, but the Navy was now manned by wooden men aboard iron ships.

Uncle Bill spent his adult working career as a coal miner after his Navy service ended. He was an avid supporter of the United Mine Worker's Union. I mention this now, because the only account by anyone pertaining to my father's later years came about as a result of the death and a following memorial tribute at Pittsburg honoring William Green, successor to Samuel Gompers as President of the American Federation of Labor. Green was also President of Ohio Mine Workers Union, President of the United Mine Workers of America, a two term Ohio State Senator, and author of the book titled Labor and Democracy. Uncle Bill was among the huge crowd on the streets when he spied my father standing in the presence of a woman. Uncle Bill proffered a handshake and said, "Hello Brother. He told me that my father declined the handshake and said, "I see someone I want to talk to," and walked away.

The woman was surprised as she asked, "Did you call him Brother?"Uncle Bill responded, "Yes he is my brother."As she shook hands with Uncle Bill, she said, "I am his wife, but he never told me that he had a brother."

Uncle Bill said, "He has had five brothers and a sister."

The woman said, "I am a school teacher and we live at Peoria, Illinois. I would like to correspond with you on a regular basis."

Uncle Bill agreed and they exchanged letters until 1959, when she informed him that my father had died. Uncle Bill did not see my father again after that day in Pittsburgh.

Since Betty and I had experienced very little 'civilian life' during our marriage and my non-airborne life in the Army was not exciting, so after two and one half years 'flying a desk' and wearing civilian suits and ties, I was homesick for the mountains of West Virginia. I was eligible for retirement, so I submitted my application, which was approved. My Unit honored me by awarding my second Army Commendation Medal with Oak Leaf Cluster, the Army's highest efficiency award.

Just after my retirement was approved, for the second time, I received orders to serve in Viet Nam, the first time being just before my assignment to the American Embassy in Korea as mentioned earlier in this book. My retirement orders predated the orders to Viet Nam, so they took precedence.

The Army was not quite finished with me, however. My records revealed that I had not only succeeded in penetrating and succeeded in gaining access to a local Pittsburg guided missile silo base using subterfuge, but had also headed two intensive Security Survey/Sound Penetration Sweeps, first of the Special Forces Base at Bad Tolz, Germany and secondly the Warner Kasern, Munich Germany.

I was furnished a round-trip plane ticket from Pittsburg to Louisville, Kentucky where I was met by a contingent of Agents from Fort Meade, Maryland.

My assignment was to perform the same examination of Fort Knox. They were loaded with essential gear sufficient to perform the mission. Upon completion of our task, I returned to Pittsburg and was never made privy of the results, because I accepted retirement within a week of my return.

There was an event during that assignment which was amusing to me. I arrived at Louisville during a late Sunday afternoon with reservations at a hotel where a WWII Armored Division were ending a reunion. Libation was much in vogue to state it mildly resulting in my getting little sleep that night. I entered the local streets at beginning of business hours that Monday morning searching for a place to eat breakfast. I found a drug store with a short-order food counter which contained ten bar-stools at the counter. Being alone, I occupied the end stool so as not to divide groups wishing to sit together. Just as my order was delivered, three young ladies arrived and sat next to me. Apparently two of them were regular customers, because one of the two cooks inquired if they wanted their 'regular.' They both said that they did.

Obviously recognizing that the third lass was new, the same cook asked, "What will you have Babe?"

She responded in a extremely broad accent, "Wal, I would like to have two aigs sonny side up or down, I don't know which."

The cook said, "You're confusing me Babe. Do you want them sunny side up or flat fried?"

Our hero replied, "Wal, I'd like to have them sunny side up, but I don't think that I can stand to look into those two yeller eyes this time of the morning."

That response elicited uproarious laughter by all of those within hearing.

While the cook prepared the girl's orders, the new girl continued talking to her friends. She said, "Today in mine and Honey's first wedding anniversary and I overslept. Honey was fully dressed and was ready to go to work. He kissed me and said good-bye. I just flew out of that bed and said, "Honey! Wait. You haven't had your breakfast." He said, "Yes, I've been meaning to talk to you about that. I never eat breakfast!"

On June 1, 1968, I retired to the Martin Farm on Little Sewell Mountain in Greenbrier County seven miles from Rainelle, West Virginia. You may have to be a mountaineer to understand the joy the soles of my feet felt when walking again upon the pristine soil of West Virginia.

# Chapter 13

# HOME AND HEARTH

My wife, daughter, our dachshund dog named Weinerschnitsel, our cat Puddy, and I arrived at my mother-in-law's house at Rupert, West Virginia during the evening hours of June 1, 1968, the first day of my retirement from the Army. We spent a few days visiting other relatives and friends, but we wanted to start settling into the task creating our new home.

I began negotiating with a local builder to construct a new house upon a fifty acre tract Cecil had deeded to me. The land contained Lon's old house where Cecil was born. I had initially asked the builder to remodel/restore the house, but he told me that it was impractical to do because it had no foundation, but rather was resting upon stacked field stone. Over the many years, the stones had sunk, thus causing the floor joists to twist and sag. The floors, therefore, could never be leveled or the walls made plumb.

In the interest of getting our furnishings out of storage in Pittsburgh, I began demolishing the old house, because its location was where we wished to place the new one. I worked mostly alone daily from daylight until darkness and soon had the space cleared. It was necessary to have a new well dug, because vandals had hopelessly plugged the existing one. Within a few weeks, the builder finished our house and the moving company delivered our furnishings. That was in stark contrast with my first arrival at that location on June 8, 1929.

I began making plans as to how I would utilize my small farm. I had three beautiful mountaintop fields and a section

173

of forest land extending to the bottom of the mountains on each side. Since Cecil continued to be mostly interested in the timber trade, he woefully neglected fence maintenance, although he continued to own beef cattle. His cattle were a menace to his neighbors' crops. Betty and I were dismayed upon wakening one summer morning and found a dozen of them relaxing inside what had been our bountiful vegetable garden. In addition, no field could be clearly viewed from a public road because of the thick hedge-rows lining them. Behind the fence rows, most of my pasture land was covered by thickets of shoulder-high blackberry briars, which greatly limited grazing space. I had plans to have a pig, a small flock of sheep, and to pasture a dozen yearling steers. There was much work to do, but I would not enact those plans until I had built secure fences around my fields. To state it mildly, my task was muscle building.

After I had enclosed the pasture fields, I purchased the animals for which I had planned. I never knew why, but Cecil had built a neat barn measuring thirty by forty five feet approximately fifty yards behind the original farm house. I was grateful that he had, because by building our house, the fences, and buying the animals, I had spent much money. Depending upon Army retirement income only, it was necessary for me to seek augmentation through civilian employment. I was granted a traveling sales position by Sears and Roebuck at Rainelle with my territory covering the western half of Greenbrier County, all of Fayette County east of the New River Gorge, and all of Nicholas County.

I was truly content to be living on the Martin farm again, but I must admit that Betty was never fond of that location serviced by narrow, winding, and steep mountain roads. The farm was approximately seven miles by each of three such roads leading in three directions before intersecting with major highways. The winter snow drifts were frequently hood deep on most cars and there was not a way to escape from the buffeting winter winds. Upon returning to Fort Bragg from my assignment to Korea, we bought a newly built brick house within a beautiful small community. We continued to own it when we moved to the Martin farm. Betty liked the convenience at our North Carolina property because of its proximity to the Army Base with its commissary, hospital, and modern shopping areas. I overrode her wishes and retired to the farm. Later circumstances dictated that I should have followed her advice. If practical, I never wished to leave West Virginia.

Our son, Rodney, surprised us by announcing that he had been medically discharged from the Navy. We knew that he was dangerously allergic to bee stings. Upon completion of advanced training with the Navy, he was advised his scheduled assignment was to be aboard a destroyer bound for duty on the Mediterranean Sea. A review of his medical records revealed the bee allergy. He was immediately discharged without recourse. He came home and enrolled at Alderson-Broadus College. Our daughter, Sue, completed eighth grade at Smoot Elementary and subsequently graduated from Greenbrier East High School at Charmco, West Virginia.

I truly enjoyed farm life, which was also shared by Puddy and Weinerschnitzel. Puddy presented us with some kittens for whom we found local homes, except for one large one we named Tater. As was his mother, he had beautiful blue-gray fur accented by pure white feet and chest area. Puddy eventually died leaving her son as the cat of the house. It became a mystery one night during an eighteen inch deep snow fall he disappeared. I had seen what appeared to be a coyote at the edge of our forest during a winter day. I can only surmise that one killed Tater.

During another winter night of twenty degrees above zero weather, I let Weinerschnitzel outside near ten o'clock PM to do whatever dogs do before bedtime. She returned to the glass door to our family room as she did each night when I smelled the odor of a skunk. I went outside via another door in order that I could observe her. Oh yes, she had attacked a skunk! We could not allow her to enter the house and, because she was an 'inside' dog with short hair, she could not survive staying outside in that cold temperature. Betty provided me an old blanket with which to wrap her. I carefully bundled her avoiding getting the odor on my clothing and carried her to the barn loft. It contained a great depth of baled hay. I removed enough bales to form a deep crypt and lowered her into it and covered her with enough bales above and surrounding it to adequately insulate her from the cold. I had to go to work at Sears the following morning, so could not help deodorize her. I bundled her inside the blanket and deposited her inside our garage where Betty and Sue used dishwater detergent and a few quarts of heated tomato juice to bathe her. They toweled her dry and made her a bed inside our heated utility room. We were pleased that she avoided skunks from that day onward.

I sought professional advice from many sources about how I could earn a meaningful income from my small tillable fields, especially without major investments in expensive farm machinery. The answers were not encouraging. Brother Max was invested in the cage-layer egg business on a large scale both on his section of the farm and through the leasing of several other chicken houses throughout Greenbrier County. He was also building a herd of beef cattle and had purchased a feed/hardware store at Rainelle, West Virginia. His children assisted him with the egg business, but much of what he did including both the production and personal delivery of eggs, was labor-intensive. He was literally 'burning the candle on both ends' so to speak.

After two years of Betty's discontent with farm life and my failure to envision an efficient use of our small holding, I decided to sell and to move to Lewisburg where Sears Roebuck had already agreed to transfer me. Max was in need of expanding his pasture land, so I told him of my plans. He was pleased that he could consolidate most of the original Martin Farm without having to purchase additional land elsewhere. We negotiated the purchase of my place and my family and I moved to Lewisburg. Max surveyed a two-acre plot surrounding the farm house and sold it shortly afterward.

We rented a comfortable home at Lewisburg and I easily blended into the Sears Roebuck Store with a much more lucrative territory than I had at Rainelle. Betty was also more content. By living there, she was in proximity of a large number of her close relatives. Rodney came home for the summer and immediately formed a new band using our basement for rehearsals. Sue applied for and was accepted to attend West Virginia Technical College at Montgomery, West Virginia where she studied music.

I had always planned to return to Morris Harvey College some day to complete the Bachelor Degree which I began during 1946. After attending West Virginia Tech two years, Sue decided to transfer to Marshal University to complete a Bachelor Degree in primary education. That would effectively move her one hundred fifty miles from our home. We were not tied to that present environment, so Betty and I decided to return to Charleston where I could complete my unfinished degree and be near enough to Sue that she could visit us during weekends. We bought Sue a small used car to use for that purpose.

Betty and I rented a small house in Saint Albans, which resulted in an approximate ten mile daily commute to Morris Harvey. I entered a seventeen credit hour assignment with all of my classes meeting before noon in order that my afternoons were free for study and to also engage in organizing an estate care business which I could operate both winter and summer. I dressed in a suit and tie in order to project a business-like appearance and set about visiting millionaire residences in Kanawha City bordering the shore of the Kanawha River and Virginia Street. The end result was that before the next summer ended, I had accrued one dozen estates as clientele.

I bought a pick-up truck, had a trailer custom made, bought a large lawn tractor with a vacuum trailer attached, a trim mower, and sundry clippers, rakes, shovels, ladders, and sprayers capable of performing professional work. I made agreements with each client to allow me to purchase gardening and lawn-care supplies at a single supply house for the necessary supplies to maintain their property without having to consult them personally for each item I needed. I utilized three-copy carbon loaded invoice pads from which I recorded and furnished an invoice to each concerned client at the end of each month.

The visible quality of my work attracted many other want-to-be customers  whom I had to turn away, because I worked alone and knew the limit to how many I could adequately serve. I became acquainted with others in the same business employing many workers. Most confided that they envied me, because they complained that they had to hire thirty workers just to keep twenty on the job daily. I did not want personnel problems that ranged from absenteeism, careless damage to customer property, destroyed and damaged equipment, failure to appear at appointed job sites, walking off the job without notice, abandoning equipment, and law suits.

I kept close contact with my clients during winter as well as summer. I cleared driveways following heavy snows, removed heavy snow accumulations from prized shrubbery, cleared gutters, and removed fallen leaves and limbs. I truly enjoyed my studies at Morris Harvey as well of the non-stressful but exhilarating exercise of my business. The rapport I created with my clients resulted in some enduring friendships.

I graduated with a Major in Geography and a Minor in History in the Class of 1975. Having begun the summer season with my lawn business, I did not seek immediate formal employment. Thoroughly enjoying what I was doing, I didn't have a care. I was awakened from sleep near 10:00 PM one night by a telephone call from Brother Max. I could detect urgency in his voice when he told me that the manager of his feed store at Rainelle had served a two-week notice that he planned to resign his job to accept work with Appalachian Power Company. Max, who had many acquaintances, could not think of one who was available for hire or to whom he would entrust the management of his store. He said that the store was such an important adjunct to his other enterprises that he could not simply close it because of their enter-dependencies. He stated that it was reluctant to ask me for such a personal sacrifice, but would I consider moving to Rainelle to manage the store until his son, Roger, could graduate from high school two years hence. Betty and I truly did not want to live at Rainelle, but I responded by saying, "Max, you are my brother. I cannot refuse your request. You locate an appropriate house for Betty and I to live in and we will be there."

Fortified with memories of all of the inconvenient moves that Betty and I had experienced throughout my military career, this one did not cause us much consternation. We would just simply go. I advertized the sale of my business complete with all of its equipment and listing of established clients. The business sold within one week.

Betty and I arrived at Rainelle and moved into the house which Max had located for us. Max briefed me about my new responsibilities and I was anxious to explore a new adventure. I did not regard that my new job was much of a challenge, but I was pleased to be helping Max as well as being back in contact with many old friends who were patrons of the feed store. Some near my age whom I had not seen for many years were wearing the scars of wartime wounds and others who were middle age during my youth wore the tracks of time upon their wrinkled faces.

I felt as though I was retreating into past ages and was once more absorbing some of the nostalgia of that Currier and Ives era when country stores and their accompanying post offices were the shopping centers for the horse and buggy generations. Those were the times when the pace of life was much slower and most people were not in a hurry. The chairs and nail kegs located on the front porches and inside the stores were places to rest and discuss current events and mountain philosophy. The country women would take advantage of a leisurely visit with the owner's wife at their residence above the store or in a comfortable house adjacent to it. The young men and boys often enjoyed horseshoe games which lasted until midnight on the sandy sides of the roads. The children were free to play games and enjoy the treats usually served to them. I was pleased that that dusty old feed store retained at least a part of the magic of those by-gone icons of rural America. The aroma of feed, fertilizer, leather goods, liniments, paint, hemp rope, pipe and cigar smoke all were there.

Our customers did not arrive on horseback, riding buggies, or with wagons as during days of old, but the traditions of bringing their entire families to town on Saturdays continued. The feed store was a place where people felt comfortable. Knife trading and whittling was a way to spend a leisurely afternoon. Long distance tobacco spitting was an inaccurate but traditional art of missing the sandbox installed as the intended target by the store owner. Re-sanitizing that area of the store was a minor inconvenience to be tolerated.

During the spring of 1978, Max's son, Roger, graduated from high school and began grooming to become manager as planed. Betty and I proceeded with our desire to return to living on our own turf, preferably in the vicinity of Lewisburg. One day when en route to a picnic at the Greenbrier State Forest at Hart Run, we saw a house for sale nearby. We contacted the real estate agent the following day and submitted our intent to buy it. Within a few days we moved into our new home.

I had retired from the Army, but I had not retired from living. Throughout our travels upon interstate highways, we had observed many neatly maintained fuel service stations and had agreed that would to be an ideal way to spend our retirement days. I was delighted when a few days after moving into our home a Texaco station located at the Hart Run I-64 exit # 175 became available for lease. I obtained the lease, attended the Texaco orientation school at Cherry Hill, New Jersey, hired one full-time mechanic, a part-time one, and launched the business.

I was determined that I was going to operate the neatest combination full and self-service station anywhere with spotless restrooms, neat interior and exterior areas, and the friendliest of customer relations. Betty was a wonderful representative of our business and helped enhance its rapid popularity. We were enjoying great success with both local and Inter-state customers. I hired one more man as dual-duty man for lubrication service and detailing. We were also fortunate to acquire two fleet maintenance customers. For two years, life was truly good.

The work was a bit confining and demanded my attention sometimes late at night when travelers on the interstate ran out of gas, wrecked, or experienced a stoppage of some type. At those times we would drive out to assist them or called a wrecker if needed. Many times stranded motorists needed lodging or directions to a place to eat. My mechanics were skilled in performing minor repairs, but I had to refer customers needing major repairs, especially after a wreck, to be referred to facilities capable of handling major problems requiring days to complete. Blowouts and flats were a constant occurrence.

A trailer's spare tire dislodged from its cage upon passing over a bridge expander joint one night just in time for it to slam through a tailgater's radiator. The trucker was unaware of the accident, but a call to the highway patrol intercepted him before he crossed into Virginia. He came back and exchanged information with the owner of the damaged car after which I took its driver to a motel.

When I hired my helpers, I made my policy clear that deserving customers were to be treated with the greatest courtesy and assistance, however I also made it understood that none of us would take any guff from any irascible punks coming off either the Inter-state or locally. One evening just before dark and I came home to eat dinner, three young ruffians wearing college football jerseys came in, blocked two of the gas pumps, and went on a rampage. Without asking for keys to the rest outside rooms they walked to their location. Two of them demolished the doors to both restrooms while the third kicked down a panel of a decorative fence between the building and the drink machines. He urinated upon the ground in sight of the highway. It was coincidental that a woman driver had run out of gas approximately two hundred feet from the station and one of my employees was assisting her. He told me that he thought war had broken out when he heard Ronnie firing his pistol. He ran back to the station in time to see two of the hoodlums prostrate upon their stomachs while he had the other one dancing to avoid being having his feet shot. I also returned in time to hear Ronnie drawl "Ed ain't going to like that." Arriving at the scene, I removed their keys from the punk's ignition and, while awaiting police to arrive, I required the offenders donate their money, jewelry, tools, and spare tire to partially cover the cost of the damage they did.

One hot summer afternoon, a man and woman driving a luxurious convertible with its top down parked beside a full-service pump. At the same instant, a woman with a child inside her car parked by a self-service pump. While her mother removed the gasoline nozzle, the child leaned through an open rear window to watch her mother. Her mother squeezed the trigger while holding it upward near the child's head and turned the pump on. Gas gushed over the child's head and also entered the car. In panic, the woman waved the nozzle randomly spraying the couple inside the convertible and destroyed a curbside flower bed before I could rush out and shut off the pump.

Pandemonium ensued. I yelled for the two mechanics to prevent additional  cars from entering the driveways, while I sent the occupants of the convertible to the restrooms and I used a nearby water hose to douse the woman and child. I yelled to my third employee to call ambulances. The ambulance crews helped calm the victims, but there was very little that I could do to rectify the situation. The woman and child were the first to leave. The occupants of the convertible stated that they were en route as guests of the Greenbrier Hotel three miles distance from my station also departed.  In an act of compassion, they did not sue me.

I had a six day hospital confinement following dual kidney surgery during the winter of 1977. The reason I mention this is to relate that I had an elderly room mate with whom I became a friend. Later during that summer he stopped by my service station. He informed me that he just been released from another hospital stay. He stated that he had just paid the cost of his treatment and had the itemized receipt which he handed to me and directed that I read item number 17. He hastened to say that he told the hospital personnel he didn't object to the charge if it was true, because it would make him famous and that he would surely be entered in the McGinnis Book of World Records.  The charge was $75.00 for prenatal care!

For reasons of which I am unaware, Texaco Corporation made the decision to withdraw all of their franchisees from West Virginia. Ironically, that decision coordinated with the 'fuel crunch' during late 1979. Texaco responded to that situation by cutting my allocation of fuel, raising its price for gas, and concurrently raising my rent. Customers purchased fuel anywhere it was available during the crisis, thus further reducing my fuel sales. Following the good will for Texaco which Betty and I had promoted, we felt betrayed by their action. We could not survive, so I paid my employees in full, also paid my utilities and concessionary suppliers, and closed the doors.

For a short while, I re-established a small lawn care service just to have something to do. Once more I was enjoying that work, when a retired friend contemplating becoming the Executive Director of a State-sponsored sheltered workshop for the severely handicapped at Ronceverte, West Virginia insisted that I become his deputy. With some reluctance, I accepted the position. The Clients' disabilities ranged from some degree of mental retardation to severe deformities. The workshop supported itself through a number of Federal contracts, salvaging metal, sorting and mailing of trade coupons, and performance of janitorial services to several nearby business establishments.

Within approximately one year, my friend resigned his position and the Board of Directors installed me to fill it. I expanded the activities of the 'Clients' services as much as the limited budget permitted and was experiencing modest success on behalf of the organization, when during the late summer of 1985, a twelve inch rainfall happened one night. I was awakened near two o'clock in the morning by the noise of the raging storm. I became concerned about the safety of the sheltered workshop and its vehicles, so I went there to investigate. I became alarmed upon discovering that the Greenbrier River was overflowing its banks. The water was rapidly approaching the workshop at the rate of four inches per minute. My first action was to call each of my assistants to come to the workshop immediately and, upon arrival, to call each of the parents of the Clients to warn them to stay at home. While awaiting my assistants' arrival, I moved all of the vehicles, including my own, to high ground beyond the threat of flooding. With the arrival of help, we began stacking tables upon which we piled everything of value we could with hope that water would not reach it. Within an hour, water began invading. I turned the electricity off and dismissed all but one male assistant. It was not long afterward that flood water broke out the upstream side windows, the force of which toppled most of the stacked tables and equipment completely defeating our efforts. We decided to evacuate for our own safety. Upon exiting the building in waist high water, we encountered swiftly floating logs filling the street in a raft-like formation as they escaped from a nearby upstream sawmill. To avoid becoming trapped or injured, we had to submerge ourselves beneath the logs and grope our way across the street to high ground.

The water began to recede the following day, so my staff and I, accompanied by the President of the Board of Directors, began to assess the damage. Two pallets of finished Government products worth several thousands of dollars were due to be shipped the date of the flood, all of our unused raw materials, all textiles including cushioned office furniture, and most of our electronic equipment was condemned and subsequently sent to a landfill. Water trapped between the walls of the building made turning on electricity too hazardous to chance before inspection by the over worked power company employees could be conducted.

After power was restored, we carefully removed our saturated business records and dried them a sheet at a time with hairdryers. By so doing, we saved the copies of our Government contracts, records of prior shipments for which payments to us were due, financial records which thankfully were not blotted, and our Personnel records. Fortunately, there were sufficient funds in our bank account to continue paying the Staff.

I suspended the attendance of the handicapped workers indefinitely pending the Board's decision as to whether the workshop would attempt to continue operation or close. The Staff members worked to clean and restore the interior of the building as best they could. A few of the dedicated Clients volunteered to help without pay in order to protect their jobs. I allowed their help only on a limited basis for fear they may become injured.

I do not easily concede defeat, so after evaluating the daunting prospects of restoring the workshop to its pre-flood efficiency, hoping to protect employment of my Staff, and to maintain the only hope for those handicapped individuals to have a meaningful life, I succeeded getting the Board of Directors to grant the workshop a probationary period to prove its ability to rebound. The workshop already was indebted to each of the four local banks prior to my becoming employed there. We had been paying monthly installments against that indebtedness prior to the flood. The Board appealed to the banks to forgive the balances owed without success.

It was evident that relief or additional funding was necessary for an interim period. Forthcoming insurance settlement would eventually replace our damaged equipment thus affording resumption of production, but the purchase of expensive raw materials had to be paid upon delivery. Shipping costs were also exorbitant. Not a single member of the Board was willing to inconvenience their self in any way. Survival was left entirely up to me.

I immediately took myself off payroll over a period nine months. Then I calculated the cost of material to replace the two shipments destroyed by the flood. I took copies of the invoices for pending payments due us for prior shipments, the amounts that we were scheduled to receive, and showed it all to our neighbor Mr. Bill Boone, President of the First National Bank of Ronceverte. I took responsibility for an agreement with him to encumber those amounts by signing a personal note to guarantee payment in full within thirty days in order to pay for the raw material needed to manufacture the replacement shipments.

With that agreement secured, I telephoned an order to our supplier at Philadelphia, Pennsylvania, obtained a scheduled pick-up date, and using the workshop's one and one half ton truck, Betty and I drove all night to get it. We returned the following day and placed the material into production. I repeated the arrangement with the bank each of three months until the workshop had returned to normal production and I secured release of my personal notes to the bank. We continued to operate in a hand-to-mouth situation struggling to survive financially, but we were almost crushed by the arrival of an agent from the National Labor Relations District Office at Beckley when he assessed the workshop with a one fifty thousand dollar fine for using the handicapped Clients who volunteered without pay to help clean the flood damage from our building. We were flabbergasted! How with any common sense could someone do that? He was totally intransigent in his zeal to fine us for violations of which we didn't have a clue. We fought for at least two months with appeals. In addition to his repeated visits, he hindered our production by interrogating personnel for what seemed endless hours. The Board of Directors negotiated with the Agent's superiors and finally settled for a slightly lesser penalty, but the results were devastating to us.

I continued my employment without pay for nine months following the flood, but the strain of trying to cope with endless problems and a virtually indifferent Board of Directors caused me to resign. There is a happy ending to this story, however, because my female assistant who replaced me had bull-dog determination over a period of several years, has finally received great support from a more cooperative Board, has obtained numerous contracts and grants, moved into a modern facility, worked completely out of debt, and now has a growing financial reserve.

# Chapter 14

# MORE HORIZONS

Now that I was a full-time 'house dude', my feet became domesticated once more. I was as free as a bird to move them throughout our five and one half acre estate performing maintenance and improvements. I built a small garden house, an imitation wishing well at the entrance of our driveway, erected a pole fence across the lawn adjacent to the highway, and attached a carport to the kitchen end of our house.

It was ironic that just at the moment that I drove the last nail into the apex of the carport gable, the eight foot aluminum ladder upon which I was standing shifted causing me to fall with my right shoulder striking the concrete floor. It had already been a 'glass shoulder' due to numerous parachute jumping injuries to it. That current injury was destructive necessitating surgery at Walter Reed Army Hospital. The surgery was a total success, but necessitated a nine day convalescence period at the hospital.

The surgeon directed that I attend therapy at ten each morning and two each afternoon throughout the time I remained there. I was pleasantly impressed when I discovered that my assigned therapist was a petite, beautiful member of the Women's Army Corps with the name tag Heaven pinned to her blouse. I told her that during my Army career, I had met thousands of soldiers, but had never seen her last name before. Thus, it became my privilege to be the only person I have ever known to get go to Heaven twice a day for nine days. I was in my room watching news on television that first evening when I heard someone at my door. When I turned to see who it was, I saw an Army Chaplin wearing Lieutenant Colonial insignia standing there.

The Colonial said, "How are you doing my Son?"

I said, "Oh Padre, I have never felt so close to Heaven as ⊺ have today."

As he turned and walked away, he said, "Bless you my child."

After returning home, I spent a brief period of convalescence before I became restless for some type of employment. It came suddenly, but not as I envisioned. The background was that Max was experiencing a major decline in business. Factors contributing to his problems were that large out of state corporate egg producers were moving into his market area selling their products cheaper than he could produce his. Adding to his predicament, the United Mine Workers initiated a major miners' labor strike which eventually lasted one hundred twenty days. Both mines and miners comprised the bulk of his market both as customers at the feed store and purchasers of his home delivery eggs. Max was loyal to his customers, so he ignored my practical advice that he   respond as did other neighborhood businesses by closing doors for the duration of the strike. Instead, he lettered a large sign and placed in a front window announcing that his store would remain open in support of the miners.  The purchases were normal, but the bulk of them were on credit which was never paid after the strike ended. I had always observed that Max was the most generous person I knew, but it was sad that many of his customers did not appreciate his compassion.

I grieved over the obvious strain he was experiencing. My worry about his plight caused me to pay him both store and home visits of consolation. It tortured him when creditors demanded payments that he could not make. He was a chain smoker, which he accelerated throughout business hours and late into nights during the crisis. The habit obviously was taking a lethal toll on his health. His wife called me in panic one forenoon minutes after his business opening time to announce that an early customer discovered him collapsed while sitting unconscious in his office chair. I met his family at the Greenbrier Valley Hospital where he was slipping in and out of consciousness. An aneurism was discovered two inches from his heart. Surgery was delayed, because his blood pressure could not be stabilized. Each time it would show some hope of increasing, the aneurism would balloon and he would lose consciousness.

In desperation, his doctor had him airlifted to a Roanoke Virginia hospital where he hoped that he could be saved. His family and ours quickly followed by automobile and, upon arrival, were informed by the doctors that they believed that his blood pressure had stabilized sufficiently to operate. That optimism quickly faded when we were informed that the aneurism had ruptured causing his immediate death at age fifty four. As a graphic testimony to how much Max was admired, it required four hours for the line of mourners to pass his coffin. They could not have imagined the depth of loss I felt upon losing the only brother I ever had.

My sister-in-law requested that I commute daily to assist her and her son, Roger, in attempting to resurrect the store's business. I complied by initiating marketing improvements and promotions. We struggled two months with cost cutting practices while facing acute undercapitalization. Common sense dictated that trying to buy time and applying for loans would only further frustration and would prolong the inevitable collapse of the business. After conducting a going out of business sale, my-sister-in-law used the proceeds to pay amounts due to suppliers, and we simply closed the doors.

Unwilling to be idle, I succeeded in obtaining a traveling job as a 'water tester' for a coal related testing laboratory at Lewisburg. The region serviced by that company covered dozens of coal mining sites spanning ten West Virginia counties and parts of north western Virginia. My responsibilities were to visit and take water samples from hundreds of designated locations along streams, seeps, and mine ponds. Many sites required weekly, others bi-weekly, and still others monthly visits. The purposes of the samples were on behalf of the Environmental Protection Agency to test the natural state of the water above and below proposed mine sites before opening them, during their operation, and a ten year follow-up examination after cessation of operations required by the West Virginia/Virginia Departments of Natural Resources regulations.

I was equipped with a Jeep, testing and sampling supplies, maps, and survival equipment, the latter because I worked every day alone in rugged isolated mountainous terrain. There were many locations which were inaccessible by vehicle, so I walked many miles upon circuitous routs with my testing equipment carried in a backpack before returning to the Jeep. At points where streams intersected, I was required to take and test up-stream samples of both and a third below. When the sites were along rivers, I was required to wade and gauge the depth and rate of flow using a flow- meter every ten feet across its width. The physical result was that I spent many days soaking wet. My feet became accustomed to encountering many slippery unseen rocks.

Due to the isolated and solitary nature of my work, I occasionally faced dangerous situations, many of which evolved through sudden changes in weather conditions. They were too numerous to describe, but one in particular merits mention. I had been testing on Shaver's Fork River one Friday with my projected time of arrival at a working surface mine site on Cheat Mountain on or near two o'clock PM. The mine headquarters was located along a dirt surface road fifteen miles west of West Virginia Route 92. My task was to establish the 'base' sampling-sites of ten seeps or natural springs each located at the apexes of ten small hollows formed vertically around the mountain side. The site was to become an expansion of perhaps the distance of a mile to an existing surface mine. The access road to the mountainous location was secured by a locked steel gate when mining personnel were absent. I made certain that the foreman knew I was there and asked him to be certain that I was not locked in, should they cease operation for the day before I completed my brief task. He assured me that he would comply.

Cheat Mountain is covered by a dense red spruce forest, whose seedling undergrowth in almost impenetrable on foot, so mush so that in clear daylight that a person can lose direction when surrounded by it. Having had experience with that difficulty before, when I parked the Jeep, fortunately for myself, I used an altimeter to read the elevation before I departed upon my trek. A heavy downpour of wet snow arrived just as I began entering the thicket. I located the nearest spring soon after starting. Once more, I recorded the elevation as I did the entire trip. It was fortunate that I did, for when I attempted to retrace my steps through the blinding snow, I lost all sense of direction and could have spent hours attempting to find the Jeep. By taking frequent altimeter checks, I found each spring in sequence and arrived at the Jeep. I was dripping wet.

I returned to the mine worksite where I found a roaring bonfire, but no workers. I rushed as best I could down the mountain road blowing the Jeep horn all the way in hopes that someone would remember that I was inside the gate. My greatest fear manifested itself when I saw the locked gate. I had approximately fifty keys on a large ring, but I tried without success to open the lock. My next glimmer of hope lay in leaving the Jeep and walking an additional half mile to the mine office, which I had visited before. There was no one there. I did have a key with which I unlocked the office door hoping to find a telephone. There was none, but I did activate a radio, but could not receive an answer.

The only recourse was to return to the Jeep and utilize my sledge hammer which contained one axe-shaped peen. I began demolishing the steel shield welded around the lock compartment of the gate. After several minutes, I broke the weld, thus exposing the lock. The lock deflected many of my blows by moving on its hasp, but after approximately thirty minutes, it fell apart. Betty always packed me enough food to survive emergency conditions. I finished eating it and began my homeward trip. Darkness had fallen and the snow was at least one foot deep and falling rapidly. Thankfully, the service road was wide to accommodate passing coal trucks, so I was not in danger of driving into Shaver's Fork River. Upon arriving at the top of Cheat Mountain traveling west where Pocahontas and Randolph County join is the location of a summertime motel where I used a coin operated outside telephone booth to call the mine foreman at his home at Marlinton.

I said, "Hello Joe. Do you have any idea who this is?

"Oh my God!" he exclaimed. "Is that you, Ed? I am so sorry. How did you get out?"

"Just let me say that you need a new lock and a welder when you return to work Monday," was my response.

I followed by calling Betty and my employer in order to put their minds at ease.

It just seemed to be the nature of my work that I encountered many other close calls involved in getting stalled in deep snows, hazardous roads, high waters, and poisonous snakes. One strip mine located near Mt. Storm was so vast that during days of dense fog or snow whiteouts, one could easily become lost. It also was on that property I would frequently see fresh bear tracks upon the paths I had to follow to complete my work. I had many near misses of deer crossing the highways I traveled during either early mornings or after dark. A short wheelbase Jeep is tricky to drive under the most ideal circumstances, but due to their tendency to spin out of control or to overturn as a result of skidding or quick steering, a driver's neck really sticks out.

One afternoon when I was testing at a working site upon Cold Knob above Little Clear Creek and the village of Crawley, I was approaching the overflow of a sediment pond containing millions of gallons of water when, without warning, a huge gap formed in its lower side totally emptying it within seconds. I recoiled backwards in time to avoid being swept away with the tumbling stones, soil, and uprooted small trees as the instant flood gushed down the mountain side.

There came a couple of days when my Jeep was undergoing periodic maintenance. The schedule of my work had to be adhered to, so my employer who had a miserly propensity to never retire a vehicle as long as it could creep, crawl, or snort, assigned me an old Ford carry-all that had an outward appearance of being an ancient refugee from a junk yard. It was a four-wheel drive vehicle that had all of the earmarks of having been exhumed from a grave. With trepidation, I launched it westward from Lewisburg via Interstate-64 when within a mile of the Lewisburg town limits, the transfer case exploded and the drive shaft came through the floor board just in front of the driver seat, penetrated the roof, and locked all four wheels into a tire blacking skid off the pavement. Other than having created an instant personal sanitation problem, I was unhurt. Becoming the beneficiary of good luck, I flagged a West Virginia State Road truck traveling toward Lewisburg and the driver dropped me off at my employer's office within twenty minutes of my previous departure.

He immediately furnished me a slightly more modern Chevy van and once more I was on my way. I retrieved all of my gear from the old derelict I had abandoned just minutes before and I traveled to Cold Knob. You should understand that off the road travel upon the terrain of that mountain is somewhat Himalayan. I received a real shock when I nosed into a road through a smooth depression with steep sides and the generator light came on bright red! While the engine was still running, I climbed to the top of the opposite side. Upon raising the hood, I discovered the battery lying upside down in a wheel-well. The battery box had been entirely eaten by corrosion, its retaining brackets were missing, and someone had previously held it into place with a few wraps of electrical tape around it and an armored wire leading to a headlight. I felt despair when I observed that all of the battery acid had spilled through a port because of missing battery caps.

Well, I learned long ago in the Army: Don't despair. When you are standing in water up to your lower lip, leaches are draining your blood, and alligators are nipping your hind side, remember your mission was to drain the swamp. Create an Army expedient! At that moment, acid was acid to me.

I had sulfuric acid in my water testing kit. I did not know what kind of acid is used in car batteries, but at that moment umpteen miles from any human assistance, I wasn't about to hike ten miles to civilization for rescue. I bound the battery into place with my belt, dumped the battery full of acid from my sampling kit, and completed my day's work. I do not know what reaction was occurring inside that battery, but I surmised there was little additional damage I could inflict upon that ancient van and its components.

Oh yes. I had a stimulating discussion with my employer while narrating into his unprotected ears what an interesting day I had.

There were very few uneventful days for me while performing my duties. There was a measure of comfort in going to long established sample sites, but it was the new ones developed as the result of increasing numbers of new mines that were opening within the territories I serviced that could present problems. One which I recall was vexing to me. I had established baseline sampling spots upon the upland area above Meadow River and traveled downward utilizing an ancient road to an abandoned farm in a narrow valley. The only evidence that it had been a farm was its only field had obviously been plowed but never harrowed. I left the road to drive to the far side of the field to reach a small stream with an intersecting smaller one flowing down a ravine. The distance was not great, but driving over the many rows of un-smoothed furrows had to be done slowly to avoid dislodging my tools and water samples.

I was crouched upon the ground while testing my first upstream sample when I heard the high onrushing speed of a Department of Natural Resources jeep. It was bounding across those furrows in such a reckless manner I wondered what kept it from upsetting. It skidded to a stop within a few feet from where I was kneeling. The driver, wearing the tan and green uniform of a game warden leaped from the Jeep with his revolver drawn and demanded, "What are you doing?"

I took umbrage at being accosted in such a hostile manner. I responded by saying, "It is none of your business!"

He persisted, "Well, what ARE you doing?"

I repeated, "It is none of your business. I am doing my job, I am here legitimately, and it is none of your business."

I continued what I was doing while he stood stymied and shuffling his feet for a few minutes, after which he copied my Jeep's license plate number and departed in the same manner in which he had arrived. I continued my day's work and returned to the laboratory as usual. My employer, who had retired from being the Director of West Virginia Department of Natural Resources, met me at my vehicle in a jolly mood, clapped me upon my back, shook my hand, and congratulated me.

He said, "I hear that you had a little run-in with a snooty Game Warden today. He was a rooky zealot who overstepped his authority. I am so pleased that you put him in his place and I told him so. Nice work Ed."

The laboratory's contracts were increasing so rapidly, I began getting assignments on a larger scale in the southernmost counties in West Virginia. Aspiring small strip mine contractors were subletting acreage from US Steel and a major natural gas corporation. Creating baseline investigations by the Laboratory's surveyors and drafting personnel necessitated that I create numerous water sample locations along the Tug Fork River, at the endless confluences of small hollow branches, and private wells. The task was overwhelming, often necessitating overnight stays in the few motels in the region. Sampling the Tug Fork River was disgusting due to the shortage of septic tanks and organized sewage plants. The farther downstream I worked, the more polluted the water became. My responsibility for testing water supplies did not concern germs, just chemicals.

There were other peculiarities that I had not observed before. First, all dwellings where constructed upon or near the flood plane of the river. Much of the land was not owned by the residents, but was secured by long-term leases from the large corporations operating in the area. The corporations did not provide infrastructure such as individual wells or water treatment facilities. Very few wells actually existed. I was amazed that many houses located at the mouths of hollows obtained their water supply by creating small dams of the hollow streams above their homes and extended two inch diameter black plastic or rubber hoses from their houses to the dams.

Since single family residences standing side by side lined the narrow river bank for miles, the geographical reality was that many of them stood at the mouths of hollows. Those residents who owned animals or poultry found it necessary to construct their barns, chicken houses, and hog sties above their houses, thus increasing pollution of Tug Fork River. The disgusting thought which haunted me was that the down-stream population was consuming the waste of their up-stream neighbors. I had to worry about my own exposure to those conditions as the increasing pollution of the river became abundantly obvious the further down stream I worked.

I would not drink the water from the area, drank only canned or bottled beverages, and ate only well-done hamburgers as my daily diet while working there. By stating this with sincere compassion, I do not disparage the residents of the area because they could not avoid the geographical and/or economic environment into which they were born. I have often wondered how much or little they benefitted from the money they surrendered in taxes.

Another terrible example of human destruction of what must have once been a lovely little valley with an equally wholesome small creek with its water rushing from surrounding mountains as it tumbled over the mossy rocks of its stream-bed was assigned to me. The devastation was unimaginable. I will not divulge the name or location of what remains of the mining town which was erected there. I shall just describe it as a place that I called Weird.

Pioneer squatters first settled into the valley, but a large coal mining company bought the land and mineral rights and opened an underground mine there during early twentieth century. They built the coal town with its company store, tract houses, tipple, shops, a saw-mill, and railroad. The former virgin forest was consumed as lumber for the houses and the small trees were cut into posts to support the mine roof. The beauty of valley was raped into what appeared as the aftermath of war. As a by product of removing the coal, a huge slag pile grew and eventually ignited by spontaneous combustion, thus adding to the yellow smoke belching from hundreds of chimneys creating a constant unhealthy haze and perpetual foul odor. The odor penetrated every aspect of existence in the town and the haze turned the exteriors of what formerly were white houses to dull gray. Illness and abbreviated life spans created a cemetery which eventually spanned the entire surface of a small hill.

Other aspects of the valley's destruction included, but not entirely limited to the water leaching into the once pristine creek from beneath the slag pile, that draining from the mine, the sewage from the residences, oil used to quell the dust from the unpaved streets, and drippings from abandoned obsolete equipment. The moss covered creek bed stones of earlier times, became a rusty brown color. Not a single bug, minnow, or amphibian survived the assault upon the stream. Perhaps due to the foul atmosphere, very few birds nested in or near Weird.

The reason I was there was the result of the removal of the last available lump of coal. The coal company hastily boarded over the doors and windows of the company store, removed its equipment including the railroad, and abandoned the population and their pets. The company simply evaporated without concern for its former employees. With what seemed to be the intention to deal the final death blow to the valley, a strip mining company applied for and received permission to move onto the high mountains above the former deep mine and, without compunction, grossly defaced them. What ultimately had become a ghost town with only a few dozen impoverished residents now was being dusted by the incessant traffic of huge dump trucks pulverizing the local roads. Considering any meaningful justification for my performing baseline tests at that location was ludicrous. Due to the state of pollution, my testing instruments could not began to record the acceptable tolerances established by the Department of Natural Resources and Environmental Protection Agency. Every sample 'went off the charts'.

There were some other peculiarities about that town which negatively impressed me. It was the only place that I had observed where people would abandon their worn out cars and appliances above their houses. Perhaps that was because their houses were built within a few feet from the creek bank.

I was also disgusted to observe that people would stand upon their front porches and toss bags of household trash into the creek which I was required to test. It was also the only place where flush pipes from toilets often emptied a few feet from where I was sampling. There was an access road leading up to the town's cemetery. In places it was blocked by heaps of old appliances, abandoned cars, and household trash, some of which encroached into the cemetery itself.

The town is bracketed by low hills along the highway in each direction where it bypasses its only single entrance. I was disgusted by the caption of a sign positioned at the town limits on each hill. Each sign was almost obliterated by open trash dumps and overgrown by scrub brush. The final degree of irony greeted travelers reading the faded letters admonishing 'KEEP (blank) AND GREEN.'

The execution of my duties exposed me to many other examples of disregard of established regulations intended to protect the environment. The most flagrant violations were perpetuated by subleases by large coal corporations to small undercapitalized upstart individuals who just barely complied with the law fully intending to rape the mountains and abandon the strip mine site just as soon as the last truck load of coal was gleaned. The State unrealistically set the bond money intended to restore the sites to their natural pre-mining state at ten thousand dollars per acre. It didn't take a PHD in mathematics to conclude it cost them less to abandon the bond money than to reclaim the damage which they had done. They simply walked away, created a new business name somewhere else, selecting another site to rape, thus leaving the State of West Virginia to pay exorbitant costs to contractors to lessen the silting of our streams. That was tantamount to the State empowering cheaters to profit by violating its laws and essentially abetting them.

My response was resignation from my job.

I became aware that the Greenbrier Hotel located three miles from our residence at White Sulphur Springs was advertising for an additional Night Auditor to replace another who was retiring. My application was accepted and I began work immediately with nightly reporting time eleven PM to seven AM. I worked at the reception desk accompanied by two other men. One was an accountant and the other was the Crew Chief. In addition to him and me registering late arriving guests, together we utilized a few hundred projected reservations to announce  statistics in advance to all sections of the hotel their forthcoming needs.

It took a few days for me to adjust to my new work hours. I am certain that I was a zombie for the first few nights, but ample free coffee helped me to cope. My coworkers were pleasant to work with. The patiently briefed me about the parameters of my job and assisted me in the preparation and printing of the reports of which I was responsible.

At some date prior to my employment, a small room adjacent to the front desk was carpeted and sound proofed for a large computer complex which was inactive because of unsolved problems. In spite of many days of repeated visits by crews of computer technicians, the problems were not solved. Many employees of various hotel departments worked night shifts. One kindly old gentleman used a vacuum cleaner nightly over a wide expanse of the areas surrounding the reception area. Although unused, he also vacuumed the computer room using the electrical wall outlets for power. It was only through the inquiry by one of the visiting computer technicians as to who had access to the room and what activity caused that person or persons to enter the computer room. Since the computer system was designed to be powered by dedicated wall outlets twenty four hours daily, it was discovered that the computer was totally confused by the janitor plugging his vacuum cleaner into one of them each night. The end result was that my job as well as others working day shifts were terminated, because two full time computer operators made our jobs obsolete. My supervisor's only remaining obligation was to be the night time guest registrar. Well, that didn't take long Folks. I was job hunting again.

I had been a member of the Lewisburg Lion's Club for some time. The members had a practice of asking members having a birthday occurring since the previous meeting to rise and to make a brief statement. I stood to render my comment, but elected to sing ' Young At Heart' instead.

When I returned to my seat, the Member seated next to me said, "Ed, I didn't know you can sing. I am a member of the Men of Greenbriar Barbershop Chorus. If you like to sing, I invite you to attend our next meeting with me."

I accepted the invitation and sang in the tenor section. Although the population density of Lewisburg, White Sulphur Springs, Ronceverte, and Alderson was not great, there was a time when the chorus had fifty members. The original group was chartered during 1950, but declined due to deaths and job transfers. Some of the charter members continued to live in the area. Greenbrier County native Tom Holbrook moved back from Newport News, Virginia during 1978 and founded The Men of Greenbrier Barbershop Chorus and was its Director until attrition forced it to disband in 1991. I have loved the barbershop manner of singing all of my adult life, having attempted without success to form a barbershop quartet in college and at various military bases. From within the Men of Greenbrier Chorus, I formed the Strawberry Wine Barbershop Quartet, having    sung for approximately five years.  Once more attrition took its toll and the chorus ceased to exist.

My singing friends, Clyde Miller and his son, Greg, owned a John Deere implement business at Maxwelton near Lewisburg. The shop foreman position was vacant, so they hired me to fill it. Everything about the job was pleasant: the owners, the parts men, the mechanics, salesmen, and hundreds of wonderful farming customers. I was treated like a member of the Miller family. As was true with life at my brother's feed store, I thoroughly enjoyed contact with the agricultural population of Greenbrier, Monroe, and Pocahontas Counties. They are my favorite kind of people. I worked for the Millers for two years, but much to my displeasure, I had to terminate because standing upon concrete floors caused    unbearable varicose vein pain in both of my legs. Upon leaving Millers, I reluctantly ended my formal working career. A few years later, I grieved over the loss of my friend Clyde because of his terminal cancer. I cherish the memories of the good times I shared with him. Thus, the evening sun sank below that horizon of our lives.

# Chapter 15

# SOME OTHER SIDES OF LIFE

Throughout my adult life, it has been my practice to stay active, to have something stimulating to do, to stay cheerful, to keep my imagination alive, and make sure that my feet didn't become idle. Precisely, I'd rather be busy than bored. Although I am retired and have held intermittent jobs of short duration, my attitude is that I never wish to truly retire. I always want to have an objective, even to the extent of having something started that I never intend to finish. I want to continue to improve and refine my life until the day I die. I also hope that at age eighty seven I continue to have a bit of boy left within me and hope to retain enough wit to cause other people to laugh and thus lighten their day.

It has been my observation that many people I know and have known seem to have grown old early simply because they have allowed their imaginations die. It appears that they forgot that they once were carefree lighthearted children. For many, that was a happy interlude filled with the joy of being alive. For others, the harshness of disappointments has captivated their personalities. They have turned their painful thoughts inward and shut out the joys of living. Each of us has suffered loss even to the extent of some loosing every thing, but each fleeting minute is gone forever and cannot be relived. One cannot relive the past. I am not qualified nor do I attempt to tell people how they should live their lives. I do recommend, however, it may be beneficial to seek those therapeutic occasions when one can join a gaggle of kids in a game of volleyball, touch football, Frisbee, or some other youth restoring activity if you sincerely seek happiness. As the lyrics of a song admonishes when suffering a set-back, 'pick yourself up, dust yourself off, and start all over again.' There also in the inference that sometimes wisdom comes 'from the mouths of babes.' Perhaps by associating with children we can recapture the zeal of living.

When seeking post retirement activities, Betty and I have felt fortunate that our daughter, Sue, lives only seventeen miles from us and, for many years, has been a teacher at the White Sulphur Springs Elementary School located three miles from our residence. She recalled the stories I read at bedtime to her brother and her when they were young. She told me that her school did not have volunteer readers and she requested me to read my stories to her class. I agreed to come one day per week. That agreement has resulted in my reading to her class and others for sixteen years. I have expanded that activity to spend one day visits to every elementary school inside Greenbrier County and many others throughout West Virginia. Those are times when I have happy feet.

The West Virginia Board of Education has furnished to me the complete listing of all schools inside the State. I make arrangements by telephone with the Principal of the school I wish to visit. If that becomes an agreement, I prepare and mail a newsletter two weeks in advance of my visit to alert both teachers and parents that I shall be reading my stories to their students. I make it my practice to arrive at opening time, stay the entire day, and read to every class. The appreciation accorded me by both students and faculty has been gratifying. There have been occasions when principals have surprised me by inviting television crews to broadcast classes while I was reading. Of course that was flattering to me, but the children also enjoyed the publicity.

In the process of writing stories, many of them remain stored unpublished inside my desk drawers waiting the time when I can afford to publish them. My life has become richly enhanced by the thousands of interesting people I have met when marketing my books. There is a growing collection of treasures in the form of complementary letters, cards, and notes I have received from students, teachers, and buyers. There are three objectives that I wish my writing to achieve: Hope that my stories encourage children to read, that my illustrations to inspire children to become artists, and that parents will revive the practice of reading to their children at bedtime.

It disturbs me that, due to the exigencies of both father and mother having to work, many families have abandoned the bonding tradition of eating the evening meal together. It is my opinion that the most important time of the day for formulating strong family cohesiveness is the span between the evening meal and bedtime. That is the time when family members seated across from each other engage in eye contact, speak of the day's activities, and analyze problems. Those are moments of staying acquainted with each other, cementing affection, and strengthening family stability. Unfortunately, too many distractions and scheduled events outside the family circle have seriously damaged or totally eliminated many traditions which formerly bound families together. I sincerely believe that the immensity of such change has weakened our Nation.

The vast decline of another family-bonding tradition is that fewer parents read to their children at bedtime. Disinterest of reading is taking a shameful toll among students today. It is almost epidemic. I hear that conclusion voiced by many frustrated teachers. Their alarmed appeals to parents about the problem often meet with indifference. Often the parents' attitudes are "that is what you are being paid to do", but it is true that children's attitudes are the reflection of what they learn at home. The cost engendered by such circumstances is devastating to our students' future in the market place and Society in general. Weakness in reading and mastering of the native language can only result in a major inhabitation to a student's future ambitions. Not for selfish reasons of profit alone, but I promote interest in reading out of genuine concern for the Country of my great grandchildren's lifetimes.

I market my books through public and school libraries, at fairs, arts and craft-shows, festivals, through filling mail orders, and at civic clubs. To date, I have not established my business on the internet. I thrill at the excitement of conducting direct sales. I enjoy eye to eye contact with customers, seeing their children, telling them my stories, and learning theirs. I thereby meet an authentic cross-section of the 'American melting pot.' The people to whom I speak span almost every spectrum of economic status, education, achievement, and interest. Although I am only a simple man, I have met some famous people, some infamous, some heroes, some hobos, some of the mighty, and many of the meek.

Melded into my enjoyable domestic life is my love of gardening. I take advantage of long balmy summer evenings to raise a variety of flowers and vegetables. In spite of all of the modern developments, man is still a product of the earth. The earth is his true home and the earth is the source of his sustenance. I have an abiding love of the earth, West Virginia in particular. Near the earth is where I want to be with my feet firmly in contact with it.

All my life, I have heard the imaginations of those who tell of how beautiful heaven must be limited of course by mans' concept of beauty. Most, when describing their concept both in speech and song refer to gold, pearls, and alabaster as possessing great beauty. I have visited the city of Rome, which must come as close to matching that description as any other city on earth. It does have some beautiful spots, but with its massive ruins dominating most of its views, it caused me to feel as though I was inside a cemetery. Italy's true beauty lay not in its cities, but in its mountains, sea coasts, and skies.

Isn't is sad to think that many people spend their lives overlooking the beauty of places such as West Virginia in hopes of going to an unproven paradise  but overlooking the one  that has surrounded them  here all along? I have spent many hours during the past thirty one years living at our residence which I jokingly call Resume Speed, West Virginia, Population Two Old People and Two Cats trekking through the mountains and forests that surround me. I enjoy the vigorous exercise and the vistas. At times I become so overwhelmed by that privilege, I have preserved some of my gratitude in verse. The following express some of my sentiments:

## NATURE'S GIFT TO ME

Gliding like a shadow at the break of dawn
With silent step the forest floor I tread upon
The tinkle of the ravine's streamlet I can hear
And a crow's  distant call falls upon my ear
My nostrils thrilling to the damp forest smells
Spirits a lift where mythical wood nymphs
      dwell

As first rays part the misty veil
When one first the passing of night can tell
Blossoms of trailing arbutus comes into view
Adorned by a single drop of sparkling dew
A mourning dove coos to its kin
And a great horned owl dozes upon a limb

The forest awakens from its peaceful night
Ground creatures scamper and birds take
      flight
I marvel at the lush flora among the rocks
And pause to view a mound of mountain
      phlox
A breeze carries a wild turkey's distant call
And stirs the trees as dew drops fall

I muse about how all of this came to be
A gift of Nature given direct to me
Costing me nothing more than to participate
At day break's dawn or during evening late
On entire days by path or stream
With mind fully alert or in idyllic dream

Throughout the year I visit that wonderland
Where an imaginary four-act seasonal play
      stage hand
Rotates the scenes each year to view
Familiar, anticipated, yet ever exciting
      and new
I never grow tired of the story line
It just grows fonder with the passing time

## MOST PRIVILEGED VIEW

To bloom a blossom where blossoms have
      never bloomed
To sing a song where songs have never tuned
To climb a mountain where no man has ever
      trod
Is to see the mystery place of God

To see a migratory flight across a misty
      morning sky
To shower a rain where only eagles fly
To meadowlark a warble over a field of
      daisy sod
Is to see the mystery place of God

To cry an infant's moment of first breath at
      birth
To astronaut a space ship outside the bounds
      of Earth
To schoolmarm a class of children upon a
      path that should be trod
Is to see the mystery place of God

To carve the fjord, to dome the cave, to sand a
      desert dwelled by nomadic sheik
To ocean a deep, or peak the summit's lofty
      peak
To nebula a constellation beyond where the
      eye can see
To sound the depths of soul where wells
      symphonic Melody

To putter a gardener's plot and flower a bed
To visit the forgotten elderly whom for years
      our Nation led
To befriend the friendless with a simple wave
      or nod
Is to see the mystery place of God


## AH! WEST VIRGINIA

When aboriginal man first blinked the
      awesome scene
The land, the sky, the streams pristine
Its page unlettered by human kind
He perceived true Paradise in his mind
Established his domain, reared the first Native
      Sons
On this great land which would someday
      become West Virginia

Across un-stepped horizons he made his path
Added moccasin print upon denizens' trail
Severed ties to his original past
No urge to retreat from Heaven prevailed
His voice blended with those of the beasts
And his species thrived upon the feast
Of West Virginia

To see the sunrise o'er the crest
Purple summits draped with morning mist
Fragrance wafted upon the breeze
Motherland's cradle rocking in the trees

From whence did that first man roam?
To claim this treasure as his home
Oh! West Virginia?

Unto this place my ancestors also came
To seek fortune, peace and fame
But most of all to breathe free
As Mountaineers forever strive to be
To share the bounty of Nature's best
To live, to die, and be laid to rest
In West Virginia

Land where great chestnuts nested bird
        and bee
Whose sturdy oaks resembled tall ship
        masts a sea
The ash, the poplar, the stately pine
Form a verdant carpet above the mines
Whose seams of coal bear witness to
Eons when other colossal forests grew
In West Virginia

O happy place of Man's acclaim
Where flowers bloom and streams abound
Where proud Pioneers gave lilting names
To poetic spots they found
Birch River, Slatyfork, Springdale,
        Monongahela
Lover's Leap, Hawks Nest, and Kanawha
Ah! West Virginia

Across its face, its furrowed brow
The Gorge, the hills, the racing streams
From the broad Ohio to the Shenandoah
To the high plateau where starlight gleams
From the days of the Delaware, Seneca,
        Shawnee, and Mingo
To the present day families who live and grow
We love West Virginia

Mountaineer baby sleep in your Mother's arms
Grow to maturity in Her Garden of Love
Preserve her forests, parks, cities, and farms
Her trails, her rivers, and skies above
Draw upon the heritage of her distant past
And provide your Children a future certain
        to last
Ah!  West Virginia!


### INDIRECT DESTINATION

Wither goest thou pretty butterfly
In erratic flight through summer sky
Beautifying life for all to see
Please spend a moment here with me

What can imitate your silent grace
Or perform such acrobatics in the sky
Effortlessly flitting from place to place
And be so pleasing to the eye

I have striven to comprehend Nature's
      mysteries deep
To learn wherein Her secret lies
Tis not revealed in the dreams I sleep
Her profound truth eludes my eyes

Oh lovely creature from lowly worm derived
What wisdom can you upon me bestow
That I may also upon your pathway glide
And be not  left standing here below

If you cannot, will not your secret say
Urgency lures you to some far-off spot
Please remember to forget me not
And come back again another day


## PATHS

Have you ever wondered who made the path
      that you walk  upon today
What ancient time, what task at hand
Caused someone to pass that way
To leave his mark upon the land
For future feet to tread
Aware of only of the past he has known
Not seeing what yet may lie ahead

Some paths are straight and narrow, others
      wide and easy
Comfort is knowing that they are always there
And you ponder their long history

The trail may wind around the bend,
The view of its end unclear
O'er hills obscured past forests, fields, and
        streams
A stroll through time when others sought
        fulfillment of their dreams

Life, too, is like a path you walk as recent
        as today
For good or bad, up hill or down
You alone must chart your way
Straight to your goal or meander in search of
        opportunity's open door
Until you find the thread tying your eternity
        to some ancient chore
It may be the path the well-worn path
Where millions have walked before

Paths it is true lead both ways
The journey's lesson learned
You have watched the sunset die, when
        morning comes it will return
The mileposts of years tell how far you
        have come
But life goes on and its end for you untried,
        you roam
And the familiar path which has brought you
        this far
Can also lead you home

# QUIET WINTER NIGHT

Nocturnal visitor from the sky
From heights where eagles cannot fly
Feather soft of purest white
No sleep disturbeth in the night
A blanket fallen upon vast terrain
O'er mountains high, ravine, and plain

From slumber I awaken to see
A magnificent scene which amazes me
My world transformed from end to end
Each twig, each shrub, each bow a bend
Each rail and wire and post
Adorned by crystalline white coats

Oh Wise Man say how can it be
That each tiny flake falls individually
To create great dunes, mounds, and drifts
That pleases my eye with Nature's artful gifts
I walk agaze with muffled step
Reminding me that I, too, am only a tiny
        speck

In reflection it seems somewhat sad to me
Never again will I view that exact winter
        tapestry
But at another time, another place
Those magic droplets will return to grace
My world once more while I sleep
Above the ground or somewhere underneath

I created the following as an adjunct to a tradition which I began thirteen years ago by climbing the steep sides of White Rock Mountain on my birthdays. The peak rises to a height of approximately two thousand and is located across a narrow valley containing Howard's Creek, the main line of CSX Railroad, and Inter-state highway 64 directly in front of our house. Access from its base is without a path through forest via a 'hog-back' ridge which alternates between forty five to sixty degrees. There are two rows of low cliffs that are not difficult to climb, but the footing of the ridgeline is difficult because of the rubble strewn hard shallow shale soil.

I have been fascinated by that mountain throughout the thirty one years I have lived at our location. During those years, I have marveled at the constantly changing view as a result of weather. I am amazed that the mountain seems to possess a personality exhibited by changes in light, darkness, snow, fog, and rain. The changes from winter dormancy to spring, the emergence of leaves and flora, the pageant of fall colors defines enchantment. I think of it as a friend who beckons "come to me. Come to me."

The view from atop White Rock is fabulous. It is clear for many miles in most directions, obscured only by other distant mountains. Upon viewing dozens of lower rounded-top of hills, in my imagination I liken them to the backs of huge prehistoric mammals grazing upon a vast plain. The beauty of the horizon where it becomes difficult to discern the separation of high mountains and the sky also encompassing the colorful panorama of farms, rivers, forests, highways, and towns greatly exceed my powers of description. I liken the closer view of the Howard's Creek Valley east from the foot of White Rock at Hart Run to the town of White Sulphur Springs and its winding green acres of golf courses as being huge salamanders whose undersides are outlined by the white sand-traps.

During the first ten years I made my birthday climbs I did it alone, much to the consternation of my wife, children, and friends who feared I would experience bodily harm. The concern intensified until I was accompanied by friends John and Linda Mugaas on my tenth birthday climb. They are avid hikers and they climbed because of their love of climbing and also it was a wonderful opportunity for them to bask in the glow of my charming personality. John took motion pictures of the event and he gave me a DVD as a gift.

The event generated enough attention the following year that I was accompanied by John, Dick Lewis, John Boyle, Monaca Foos, and Nan Morgan. That resulted in a fun-filled experience and another DVD. The footing on that occasion was especially slippery resulting in frequent falls. Once more I demonstrated that I am often as ungraceful as a pregnant yak.

On my eighty-seventh birthday, I was accompanied on the climb by my youngest granddaughter, Jana Marie White. Aside from being a registered nurse and pursuant of a Master's Degree, she is an accomplished mountain climber and deer hunter. My daughter, Sue, had planned to accompany us, but had to entertain visitors.

After reaching the summit upon one birthday when I climbed White Rock alone, I sat upon a grave like mound of dirt approximately eight feet long which pointed east and west. A slight breeze had accompanied me throughout the climb. I wished to spend an hour in reflection and absorbing the marvelous view. The bright sunshine had worn through the darkness and an early morning fog during which I had began my climb. I was now comfortably warm and soon fell asleep. Being totally relaxed, I had the following memorable dream:

# THE WHISPER

The breeze seemed to carry a whisper and the speaker seemed to say "Rest here beside me for a while my friend. I have waited a long time for you to return to the mountain. You cannot see me, but I am the spirit of an ancient Indian buried beneath the mound upon which you are sitting. You are welcome here. Today you are eighty three, but your great great great great grandfather was a mere lad when I was buried here. I think that you love this spot as much as I always have since the days when I was a Seneca Indian youth. Many moons have passed since that time. You are now a child by comparison, but you are growing into the age of wisdom. Wisdom is often only the learning of simple truths. You must have noticed that my grave points to east to west. It is symbolic in recognition that the sun, which regulates all things upon this earth, begins each day by rising in the east and closing each day by setting in the west. Between those two extremes, the wise man makes an honest endeavor to make life worthwhile  for himself, to be a benefactor to others who desperately need help, and to try to bring to an end man's cruelty to man. Final wisdom has taught me that when man has viewed enough suns to fulfill his allotted time, he must surrender his space on earth to make room for the newly born. It has always been true that when an ancient one departs a new child is born. Many people believe that the years which you have been counting were predicated upon the birth of a baby boy over two thousand years ago. Live your years  honorably. I have spoken."

When I awakened, the breeze was no longer blowing and I pondered what I thought I had heard. The admonition

seemed to have been given to me by a whisper. Deeply moved
by the experience, I reluctantly began my descent.

Subsequently, I wrote the following:

## WHITE ROCK MOUNTAIN

An Inter-state Highway now passes his door
Where laurels and sycamores lined the glen
    before
White Rock Mountain a mighty peak
His ancient feet bathed in Howard's Creek
Home to red eye, bass, and trout
And chirping frog-lets when spring breaks out

Sitting majestically upon his massive throne
Face bearded with oak and stately pine
Rills etched into his rugged steeps
A lap-robe of violets, dogwood, and
    rhododendron
Drapes his knees, the gales of winter gone
Grapevines into his vineyard creep

A faithful sentinel he stands always there
As seasons come and seasons go
Impervious to winter's frigid air
Hoary frost white across his brow
No rushing streams, no nestlings now
His coat of snow the purest white
Silence his lone companion during the night

He yearns for lovely Greenbrier Mountain
    across the vale
The love of his heart, she is so graceful and gay
Separated by the narrow valley at their feet
So near yet so far away
No force on earth can they avail
Two lovers who can never meet

Love notes the birds between the two
    exchange
Avowing faithfulness for all time
Blowing kisses upon the breeze
And praying for that union so sublime
When lovers at last embrace
Forever face to face, when Love does not
    decline

The small park named the Greenbrier State Forest at Hart Run is a former Civilian Conservation Corps (CCC) base camp located less than two miles from my residence. It contains eleven rental cabins, a camp ground, a large swimming pool, and two picnic shelters. It also contains eight trails rated from moderately difficult to easy ranging in length from one and one half miles to seven. The trails accommodate hikers, trail bikers, and riders of horses. During the past thirty one years, I have walked thousands of miles alone upon those trails. I have always wished that I could share those pleasures with Betty, but she has permanent damage to her back resulting from a head-on collision many years ago. She can enjoy only an occasional drive or a picnic in the park. One evening at dusk several years ago, I exited a trail and met an author friend, Belinda Anderson, also having completed a hike of another trail. I had no idea that she was also fond of the Park. We expressed surprise upon seeing each other. I inquired if she walked there frequently. She said she did. I asked if she would enjoy having someone as a hiking partner. I still hike alone several times each month, but have teamed with her many times. Also since the occasion when she joined the others on my birthday climb 2007, Monaca Foos, who owns and operates the Wiley House Bed and Breakfast at White Sulphur Springs has joined me tramping upon the more difficult trails both inside and outside the park.

On a few occasions, I have enjoyed a few hikes at sites of their choosing with my friends John and Linda Mugaas and John and Floy Boyle. We organized a day trek on one segment of the Appalachian Trail two summers ago, but, due to unforeseen circumstances, could not keep plans to visit other segments since that time. We are, however, planning to do that during the summer of 2009.

# Chapter 16

# FACING THE SUNSET

I knew at the outset of this book that I could not trace every step, but I hope that I have not made too many compromises. As you must have gathered, I have no plans to slow my pace or to park my feet any time soon. There are  many places to see and things to do abandon my interests now.  You must have also become aware that I am a simple man and that my life has not been very complicated. That in itself lessens potential for hypertension.

Before I lose the final three hairs from my former heavily covered scalp, I have planned a to-do list as follows before time forces me to park my feet:  I have a  title for a novel I plan to write after I have published Feet. I am anxious to start it. I want to hike several segments of the Appalachian and Allegheny trails, to hike upon old forgotten West Virginia log roads and trails, and to make one more parachute-jump. I have planned for years to drop off at the mouth of some remote site in one of the Rocky Mountain States and backpack up a rugged canyon with my son and to  use an old aluminum dishpan I have saved for thirty years to pan for gold without caring if we find any or not. I just want to go through the motion to say I have done it. I want to read to the students at a hundred more schools and to sing again in a barbershop quartet. I want to make more new friends and to spend time with those I already know. I want to visit nursing homes to read my children stories to revive nostalgia among the residents of their and of their children's childhoods.  So many times they must feel that their lives are blighted and forgotten, that they are no longer considered to be important. Several years ago those thoughts occurred to me which resulted my writing of the following:

## FADED FAYE

Sitting alone inside a tiny room
Sunset shadows creeping across the walls
Feeling abandoned and trapped inside a
       live-in tomb
Demented yelling of a neighbor down the hall
Behind one-way doors with nowhere to go
Foul stench permeating the air like blight
Abject boredom a constant foe
Fingering her gown, Faye contemplates
       another dreary night

Her husband and friends have gone to
       their rewards
Now she is inventoried among humanity's
       forgotten souls
She hardly notes the hours the town clock tolls
Dreams of her youth in memory stored
Gaye was elegant in her younger days
With a bewitching smile and auburn hair
Had a graceful stride and winsome ways
With dancing eyes and skin so fair

An infrequent letter arrived today
With a photograph of her daughter's family
       shown
"It's been ten years since we moved away

Thought you would like to see how the kids
     have grown
Mother I know you will enjoy the news
My husband got tenure in the Department of
     Philosophy
A dream job at Princeton University
So we will celebrate by taking a fabulous
     Caribbean cruise

You should be proud of your grandson Brad
He looks so much like my dear departed Dad
He may call you from his European tour
When he has time, he will visit you for sure
And little Faye your sweet name sake
Had a 'lark' at Lauderdale's spring break
This summer she is studying interpretive
     dance
At a 'Left Bank' studio in Paris, France

I'd love to see you if I could just find the time
You can't imagine how demanding my social
     obligations be
It is such comfort to know that you are treated
     kind
In that nursing home in rural Tennessee
My family fully realizes that we did not
     succeed alone
We simply could not have done it without you
Appreciated the proceeds of your business,
     farm, and home
That provided the means to see us through

In closing I send best wishes from us all
Hoping this finds you in good cheer
If time permits, we plan to visit you sometime
     next fall
Or at latest early the following year
Fond memories keep our love alive for you
In appreciation for your generous sacrifice
For Mothers do what Mothers do
And you are so special in our lives

Mom, have you noticed how fast time flies?
The past ten years have just whizzed before
     our eyes
A late party last night has me moving slow
Now I must rush before the postman goes
I haven't packed for our trip across the water
But I wanted to say I have not forgotten you
After all a cheerful letter is the least I can do
So I remain forever your only child,
Signed:      Your loving daughter"

Above all else at the coming of New Year 2009, as always I avowed a new  to demonstrate to Betty, my wife of sixty three years, that my love for her grows with each passing day. I will work to remove stress and to make her life as pleasant as possible. She has been a perpetual blessing to me, to our two children, and two grandchildren. She has been the consummate wife, mother, and grandmother. Also, no matter where my feet have taken me during our past sixty three years together, she has always accorded me total support. As was the admonition contained in our wedding vows, I promise 'to love, cherish, and support her through good times and bad, through sickness and health, for better or for worse, keeping myself unto her, and abandoning all others until death do us part.' Keeping that promise has been easy for me because of her gentle personality and her devotion to me. Our marriage has blossomed where so many others have failed.

I am amazed at all that she has done throughout all of those years to keep me content, to wit: Cooking my meals, doing my laundry, keeping a clean house, shopping for my needs, listening to and talking to me when I needed comforting and support, laughing at my jokes, honoring my friends, making sure that I dress properly with matched colors, and acting a perfect lady both at home and in public. An adage states that behind every man stands a good woman. The originator of that must have had Betty in mind. I am certain that I could have never been happy with anyone else. I think that I understood that the first time I saw that same pretty little brown eyed girl. She was five years old and attended a house party with her parents as guests of my foster grandparents. I did not see her again until she registered as a freshman and I as a sophomore at Smoot High School during September 1937. On August 12, 1990, the day of our Fiftieth Anniversary I presented the following verse to her:

## MY PERPETUAL VALENTINE

The first time I saw you, you were five
A beautiful child with big brown eyes
"Puppy Love' in those early days
Grew with time to full blown blaze
During elementary grades we never met

But you were a song that I could not forget
Fate worked its spell and did its part
And you became my High School Sweetheart

During those carefree days our hearts
     entwined
With love sincere to last through time
Of days unnumbered and years untold
We pledged to forever each other hold
Whatever Fate befalls or upon us bestows
Along the path as our true love grows
Unwavering and faithful throughout Life
Some day to become husband and wife

Clichés say with absence the heart grows
     fonder
Frustration will test the plans we ponder
Trails through Life make many turns
But like ships at sea the shore lights burn
Good things come to those who wait
So when you are right do not hesitate
War time put our plans on hold
Uncertainty cast us into its unpleasant mold

But came the day when we could stand
In sight of all hand in hand
To vow forever to love and cherish
To keep Love's flame alive, not let it perish
Fifty good years has spread the time
Our two children made our Lives sublime
Dreams fulfilled vast as the oceans
In our Home of Peace, Respect, Devotion

Our Friends now speak of twilight years
But we beam with pride and shed no tears
Beautiful grandchildren add cheer to our days
Our ultimate joy as our hair turns gray
I thank Providence for our near perfect health
The Love I have known and my greatest
      wealth
My Angel, my Friend lovely and kind
My Dearest perpetual Valentine

I truly believe that Betty's decorum and genuine friendliness has enhanced my status in business and among our friends. I also believe that my good health is due to a great degree by of our long happy marriage. She is an accomplished cook which certainly must influence my health. Perhaps the gallivanting of my happy feet are also attributed to that.

Perhaps it is wise for me not to be too euphoric about my indestructibility, l wrote the following to poke some jest at my mortality:

## IF IT WORKS, REJOICE
## IF NOT, GOOD LUCK

Welcome to my age of creaks and cricks
Of squeaks and squawks and spasmodic ticks
Malfunctioning innards that give me fits
A wacky back and balky joints that click
And sound when I walk like breaking sticks
The era when my overworked hair grows thin
Dull red eyes so dry, no tears within
And I sympathize with my peers

As great clumps of hair grow out our ears
Gone are the days when ladies swooned
When I, their beloved, entered a room
Now they recoil when I flash a toothless grin
Aghast to see the end of my nose can touch
        the the point of my chin
Years ago I was the Dandy of the PTA
Before senility came my way
Now it is a challenge for me
To play a brisk game of dominoes at AARP
But, just like the Old Gray Mare ain't what
        she used to be
During the days of the horse and buggy
Thus in peril of becoming an Old Has-been
I'm in pretty good condition for the shape I'm in

So now this saga must come to a close. Just as each of us has walked many paths and left many tracks behind, I hope we see many more sun-rises and that I meet many of you upon the trail. I hope that each of you have humored me by reading the pages of my book. It has always been my imagination when writing a story that I am sending it as friendly letter to a dear friend and hope that it is interesting enough that he or she will be glad to receive it. It would be rewarding to me to know if you enjoyed this one.

Best wishes,
James E. Martin

CPSIA information can be obtained
at www.ICGtesting.com
Printed in the USA
FFOW03n1420091015
17575FF